A FELLED TREE SPROUTING

Essays on the Nature of the Church and the Gospel

Parchment Press

471 Sulphur Springs Road
Hiddenite, NC 29636

ISBN-13: 978-0-9818641-3-6

First Printing 07.15.2010

PARCHMENT PRESS
471 Sulphur Springs Road
Hiddenite, NC 28636

CONTENTS

THE RISE AND FALL OF THE EARLY CHURCH

THE FOUNDATIONS OF THE GOSPEL OF THE KINGDOM

SALVATION IS A FREE GIFT, BUT WHO IS IT GIVEN TO?

THE RESTORATION OF ALL THINGS

THE RISE AND FALL
OF THE
EARLY CHURCH

*Have you ever wondered why
what calls itself the church today
bears little or no resemblance to the church
you can read about in the book of Acts?
Or have you ever wondered
why so much blood has been shed
over the past 1900 years in the name
of the Prince of Peace?*

*The articles in this section shed light
on these mysteries through the amazing analogy
of photosynthesis, the means by which
the energy of the sun sustains
all life on this planet.*

THE COLORS OF LIFE AND DEATH

The eyes of all look expectantly to You, and You give them their food in due season. You open Your hand and satisfy the desire of every living thing. (Psalm 145:15-16)

Nevertheless He did not leave Himself without witness, in that He did good, gave us rain from heaven and fruitful seasons, filling our hearts with food and gladness. (Paul the Apostle in Acts 14:17)

The beautiful poetry of the Psalms, echoed in Paul's words in the New Testament, expresses the detailed care God has for all of His creation, from the least of creatures to the highest: mankind. And "satisfying the desire of every living thing" begins with the sun's warmth and light reaching the earth day by day. Its awesome outpouring of energy, powered by the nuclear furnace within, boiling over 93 million miles away, is captured by the gentlest of living things, the green plant. There, on land and sea, the sun's energy becomes the means by which green plants grow. Through the marvelous handiwork of God, these in turn become the ultimate source for the food of all other living creatures. And in doing so, the green plants and the sea's plankton also supply the world with a continuous source of fresh oxygen.

This process, called *photosynthesis*, produces glucose, the basic sugar of life, which the plant also converts to cellulose, the structural material of plants. And the glory of it is that most plants produce more glucose than they need, storing the rest as starch and other carbohydrates in the roots, stems, leaves, and fruit. These reserves can be drawn upon for extra energy or to grow more. The prodigious amount of extra produced by photosynthesis in plants is hard to grasp:

> Each year, photosynthesizing organisms produce about 170 billion metric tons of extra carbohydrates, about 30 metric tons for every person on earth. ("Photosynthesis," <u>Encarta 2000</u>, Microsoft Corporation)

One of the colors of life, then, is surely the soothing green of plants. They enable man to breathe fresh air, and to burn fuels the many ways he does, and yet never run out of oxygen! It is continually replenished by the process of photosynthesis, which converts six molecules of water and six of carbon dioxide into one molecule of sugar (glucose) and six of oxygen, the stuff we breathe. In the tens of thousands of cells making up just one green leaf are forty to fifty chloroplasts each, complex structures containing millions of chlorophyll molecules. They give plants their green color and, most importantly, capture the sunlight which provides the energy for the plant to build with. When the plant converts that solar energy into chemical energy, it is ready to take carbon dioxide out of the air and water up from its roots to build and to sustain the plant with. And from its excess, the green plant feeds the entire living world on the surface of this planet!

Where that process of photosynthesis fails and the chlorophyll no longer receives the light of the sun, then a host of other natural processes are ready to turn the dying matter into compost, returning its nutrients to the soil, thus completing its life cycle. Indeed, chlorophyll molecules are continually being used up and replaced throughout the growing season. When autumn approaches, the rate of replacement slows, and the other pigments, previously hidden by the dominant green of the life-giving chlorophyll, come to the fore, and the beautiful foliage of autumn is on display. But when stress, infection, or weakness shuts down the life-giving process, the once-vibrant life of the plant becomes the prey of mold, rusts, mildews, smuts, mushrooms, and yeasts. This is particularly noticeable in energy-rich plants such as corn, which are highly desirable targets of such destroyers. They are either parasitic in nature, feeding on the living plant, or saprophytic in nature, feeding on the dead or decaying plant.

None of these destructive agents require or benefit from the light that sustains the healthy plant. They do not respond and turn to the sun, as healthy plants do. Their colors are whitish, grey, black and blue, standing in stark contrast to the vivid greens that chlorophyll molecules give plants. Their life is not constructive, feeding the plant and the rest of creation, but destructive, feeding themselves at the expense of the once-healthy plant. They mar and corrupt its beauty, end its useful life, transform it into a source of further corruption until the whole crop is infected, and then lie in wait as spores for another opportunity – another field of productive plants – to destroy.

There is much to learn from natural science that can open our eyes to what is happening in the spiritual realm. Western science did not begin as the triumph of atheism, which is how it is often presented today. Rather, it was the attempt by men to understand the mind of God as revealed through His works in creation. Long ago, the Savior of mankind used the "commonplace" miracles of the natural world to give men understanding of what was at work in the unseen spiritual realm around, and even within themselves. He made many comparisons between the Kingdom of God and everyday things, such as bread rising, seeds growing, and the colors in the sky. He was trying to help men see what could not always be seen merely with their own eyes and their natural understanding. The same lessons are still present in creation today for those with eyes to see and, most of all, ears to hear. ❦

THE GLORY OF THE EARLY CHURCH

L ike a well-tended garden, the early church in Jerusalem took in an abundance of the light of the Son and produced abundant fruit of the Spirit — love, joy, peace, patience, longsuffering, kindness, goodness, faithfulness, gentleness, and self-control.[1] It was the same way in the churches the apostles established throughout the Roman world.[2] Like a healthy plant, they produced this fruit through responding to the light, as the Apostle John spoke of repeatedly in his first epistle:

> He who loves his brother abides in the **light**, and there is no cause of stumbling in him. He who hates his brother is in **darkness** and walks in darkness… (1 John 2:10-11)

It was the light of revelation that John was talking about, the revelation that comes to those who love Messiah enough to obey Him.[3] It was the same light from heaven that the Master confirmed in Peter when he proclaimed Him the Messiah.[4] The light of the Messiah's life in His

---

[1] Galatians 5:22-23   [2] 1 Thessalonians 2:14   [3] John 14:21,23
[4] Matthew 16:17-18

disciples, emanating from His love poured out in their hearts,[5] produced the predictable response of *love for the brothers*. This was not a mystical love expressed in words alone, but a real love expressed in the very practical, real ways that John detailed in 1 John 3.[6] According to John, one who did not freely share "the world's goods" did not possess God's love, but was only fooling himself. True love is shown in the kind of sharing seen in Jerusalem in Acts 2 and 4, where all things were held in common and no one lacked *anything* he needed.[7] Anything less than this was not

true love — such as holding on to one's own life and possessions. God judged this very seriously in Jerusalem in those early, sincere, and pure days of the first-century church.[8]

Their self-sacrificing love, expressed in both the big and small ways, was noted with wonder by the world around them. They were even said to have "turned the world upside down."[9] This quality of love expressed in their everyday life was proof that they were living and walking in the light. Or to put it another way, they lived their lives as though Yahshua[10] were living in their communities in bodily form, as though His eyes were upon them and the grace of His immediate presence was available to them.[11]

Their willing hearts were continually responding to the teachings of the apostles, just as chlorophyll continually responds to the sun. The natural result was that they became more and more like their Master, Yahshua the Messiah.[12] He had made the great promise to those who loved Him (which is to say, those who *obeyed* Him) that He would reveal Himself to them:

> *"He who has My commandments and keeps them, it is he who loves Me. And he who loves Me will be loved by My Father, and I will love him and manifest Myself to him." (John 14:21)*

---

[5] John 1:4; Romans 5:5   [6] 1 John 3:14-18   [7] Acts 2:42-47 and 4:32-37
[8] See the story of Ananias and Sapphira in Acts 5:1-11.   [9] Acts 17:6 (KJV)
[10] *Yahshua* is the Hebrew name of the Son of God; see *The Name Above All Names* on page 151.   [11] They could *confess* that He was among them, 1 John 4:2
[12] Matthew 28:19-20; Acts 2:42

The Analogy of Chlorophyll

Each plant's chlorophyll harnesses the vast energy of the sun, enabling it to grow, mature, reproduce, and withstand disease. That vast energy in the physical world may be compared to the Word of God in the spiritual realm. Those who respond to it prove they have the same spiritual "chlorophyll" as the early church. Naturally, they will bear the same fruit the first disciples did. The secret of the glory of the early church was this: The Savior and His disciples had the *same* heart to do the will of their Father in heaven. This is what gave them the glory to be one as He prayed the night before He was crucified.[13] This willingness is the "chlorophyll" that continuously and fruitfully responds to the love/light of the Father. This heart passes on to the rest of the body all that it needs to grow, mature, reproduce, and resist infection, disease, and spiritual death.

Yahshua was the seed of life from which they came, which fell to the ground and died and so did not remain alone,[14] but filled the hearts of many with love and hope. He showed His love to the uttermost, even going to the cross for them in obedience to His Father.[15] Receiving this heart is what enabled His disciples to receive the grace and power *to do* the Father's will. They were truly linked to their God, and as a germinating seed explosively grows, they enjoyed in those days the growth that comes from God.[16]

As they responded to God's light in the gospel, they continued to express it through outspokenness in their gatherings, where all were free to share, not just a specialized, highly educated few.[17] As James would write many years later, taking care of its widows and orphans was a sign of whether a church was actually connected to God.[18] But this standard was actually set in the very beginning of the Church, in Acts 6, where taking care of the widows and orphans was a matter of the highest council and importance — so important, in fact, that it would have taken the apostles away from their ministry of the Word to serve if no one else had been appointed to serve.[19] They knew the Father's heart towards the widows and orphans as expressed in Psalm 68:

> *A father of the fatherless, a defender of widows, is God in His holy habitation. God sets the solitary in families; He brings out those who are bound into prosperity; but the rebellious dwell in a parched land. (Psalm 68:5-6)*

They did not want the communities they had begun to end up as a dry and parched land, no longer moistened by the showers of grace from heaven above. It is only the rebellious — those actually disconnected

---

[13] John 17:20-21   [14] John 12:24   [15] Matthew 26:39; John 20:17   [16] Colossians 2:19   [17] 1 Corinthians 14:1,26,31   [18] James 1:27   [19] Acts 6:1-7

from the God of Heaven — who ignore the widows and orphans in their midst. As James would write many years later,[20] such people also do not bridle their tongues, but talk on and on:

> If anyone among you thinks he is religious, and does not bridle his tongue but deceives his own heart, this one's religion is useless. Pure and undefiled religion before God, the Father, is this: to visit orphans and widows in their trouble, and to keep oneself unspotted from the world. (James 1:26-27)

Preamble to Christian History

The epistle of James would, sadly, be the preamble to the awesome and terrible Christian history which followed the days and acts of the apostles. The epistles of the New Testament exposed the problems of the early churches (which the Holy Spirit evidently wanted us to know about), as well as the revelation given to those who had received the good news.

Far from being either a rigorous statement of theology or a glorious march through its early history, the New Testament chronicles what can only be described as a continual spiritual decline. By the time James wrote his epistle, the story was virtually over, the light of revelation extinguished, and the fire of love down to a few coals in the hearts of the few sincere. The grave warning signs were recorded not only in the letters to the churches in Revelation 2 and 3, but in many other places as well, from the first letter to the Corinthians on.

The following articles in this publication discuss many of them which, if one reads the New Testament with open eyes, are both shocking and revealing in their portrayal of the decline, even the death of the young church. Selfishness, immorality, greed, Gnosticism, and rebellion against God's authority in the apostles and prophets were all fatal wounds, culminating in the takeover of the church by the Nicolaitans — the clergy. They were a grim representation of the deeply stained condition of most in the churches. Their garments ended up the color symbolic of death and evil — *black*. With them, night had come when no man could do the works of God, just as Messiah prophesied in John 9:4.[21]

If you desire to be set free, not only from this evil religious system, but also from the deep effects of unbelief on your soul, read on. We have found the antidote to the silence of the churches in which only the educated few speak. It is the thankfulness of those truly saved by the blood of the Lamb, who overcome by the word of their testimony, and who do not love their own lives unto death. They have something better to love — His life! ✻

---

[20] See *The Insurgent* on page 21 for more about the Epistle of James. [21] See the article *Nightfall* on page 33 for an explanation of this prophecy.

THE FADING
OF THE LIGHT

The physical world often gives us insight into the unseen, spiritual side of creation, just as creation itself proclaims the glory and power of its Creator. The Living Bible very clearly describes this knowledge:

For the truth about God is known to them instinctively. God has put this knowledge in their hearts. From the time the world was created, people have seen the earth and sky and all that God made. They can clearly see his invisible qualities — his eternal power and divine nature. So they have no excuse whatsoever for not knowing God. Yes, they knew God, but they wouldn't worship him as God or even give him thanks. And they began to think up foolish ideas of what God was like. The result was that their minds became dark and confused. (Romans 1:19-21)

The Apostle Paul was trying to help us see that the things in the world around us reveal important aspects of what is unseen, but still very real. For example, there are a host of diseases to which we, animals, and plants are susceptible that come from mildews, spores, and viruses. Some can hardly be described as living organisms, as they are so persistent, so enduring, and so very dark in their nature. These diseases should cause us to stop and think. Are they telling us something we should know? They wait for times of weakness and stress in order to invade, take over and, if possible, turn the host into a great factory for producing more of their own useless, destructive kind. Finally, worn out, the unfortunate host dies under the burden, deprived of nourishment, light, and life.

Smut is a good example of this, in regards to both the fungus which infects weakened plants, and the moral degradation which pervades modern society. No one in his right mind would eat smut-infected corn, yet in some circles it has become a delicacy.[1] In the moral analogy, an upright person would not give his soul over to spiritual smut, yet many falter under the temptation to do what they know is wrong, and even delight in it. Unless one promptly and deliberately turns away from it, the nature of evil begins its work in his soul, just as smut saps the life out of the plant, eventually destroying it.

Eventually, a person's taste buds can be trained until what was once revolting becomes a delicacy. He puts away the revulsion he naturally feels at eating the twisted, discolored masses of spores (i.e., corn smut) just to have a new and perverse pleasure in life. In the moral analogy, that is like silencing the voice of one's conscience which is telling him not to do something that hurts another person. The toll of "smut" weighs on the body and taxes the soul, no matter how much one enjoys it. In the end, as with any sin, it takes away the life of its possessor.

The Infection of the First Communities (Churches)

Something like the invasion of smut happened in the spiritual realm many years ago, as the light faded in the early church. In the beginning, the Holy Spirit enabled them to do what has seemed impossible ever since — put away the obvious deeds of the  flesh, such as division, greed, and war, and instead, by His grace, live *together* in harmony and peace.[2] This was the faith they received, the persuasion and the grace that they could do what was otherwise impossible for men to do.[3] But Christian theology now proclaims it *is* impossible, yielding to the overwhelming weight of historical evidence that the flesh really is mightier than the Spirit.[4]

[1] See *The Splendor of Smut* on page 15   [2] Acts 2:44-46   [3] This is the faith "once for all received" of Jude 1:3, not a set of doctrinal statements anyone living any kind of life can subscribe to and say they believe.   [4] For instance, although the

And it was impossible for the infected, disease-ridden, and smut-laden body the early church became, which mutated beyond all recognition in just a few centuries from its beginnings.[5] Since then, that dead body has filled the world with her spores of mistrust, suspicion, and unbelief, teaching that obedience to God's word is not only impossible, but is to be considered an active evil called "works salvation."

However, it was not always so. The first-century church had been the bride-to-be,[6] whose corporate life together, gathered in communities following the pattern of the one in Jerusalem, was the light of the world.[7] With that light, she was bringing salvation to the ends of the earth (as they knew it then).[8]

As the willingness of the many faded, as silence began to fill the gatherings (except for the emerging clergy), and as more and more disciples took thought for themselves, no longer freely sharing whatever worldly goods they had with one another, the light began to dim. As men began to speak in the flesh, seeking their own glory, the light of revelation ceased to shine upon them in their gatherings. The gates of the unseen realm began to prevail over the church.

That spiritual light only shone on those with the glory of their Master, the glory to be one as He and the Father are one.[9] In the end, there were only a few who still had the glory of their Master. It departed as their unity crumpled in the face of things like showing favoritism to the rich, not heeding the cry of the poor and hungry in their midst, and not

Pilgrims viewed the early church as the pattern to be restored, and attempted to do so in the new world, they failed. See the article *Till Kingdom Come*, on our web site. [5] "Between the years AD 100 and AD 500, the Christian Church changed almost beyond recognition. ... [At first] The organization of the church was still fluid...there were no creeds to be recited, no set forms of worship... [By AD 500] The worship of the church was entirely liturgical with fixed, set forms of prayer..." Tony Lane, *The Lion Book of Christian Thought* (Lion Publishing Company, Batavia, Illinois, 1984), page 8. [6] 2 Corinthians 11:2; Ephesians 5:25-27 [7] 1 Thessalonians 2:14 [8] Paul's words in Acts 13:47 were taken from Isaiah 49:6. Obviously, the knowledge that the apostolic ministry was to raise up the twelve spiritual tribes of Jacob to bring about the promises made to the fathers, as Paul spoke of in Acts 26:6-7, has been lost, along with many other things that need to be restored in the last days. [9] John 17:21-23

keeping themselves unstained from the world.[10] This was in stark contrast
to their beginnings when the apostles were ready to stop teaching rather
than let the cry of the neglected widows and orphans ascend to heaven,
for that cry would have condemned them before their God.[11]

Early in the second century, when James wrote his epistle,[12] he could
see where their friendship with the world was leading them — to wars
and murder in order to obtain the things they lusted after. And in this,
James was certainly a prophet, as Christian history abundantly shows. The
common life of the early believers was history by then, a part of their
now-legendary beginnings, meaning that as far as the lives of the people
were concerned, Acts 2 and 4 may as well have been a myth. It was no
longer the living experience of believers *everywhere* or even *anywhere*.
Another gospel, another Yahshua was being received, as Paul had already
warned. They eventually even changed His name, as most modern
translations call Him by a name that would have been foreign to His
ears.[13]

> *For if one comes and preaches another Jesus whom we have not preached,*
> *or you receive a different spirit which you have not received, or a different*
> *gospel which you have not accepted, you bear this beautifully. (2*
> *Corinthians 11:4)*

After Paul's warnings, the cries of the other apostles and prophets,
such as John and James, were also ignored.[14]

The beginnings of the transition to another Jesus and another gospel
and another Holy Spirit are easily found in the Scriptures, but not readily
recognized for what they are. To do so would be to question the validity,
not just of Christianity past (the horrors which many recoil from), but
also of Christianity today as the vehicle of God's salvation. Yet to
embrace the Christian gospel as the truth, one must repudiate the life and
practices of the early churches as recorded in the New Testament. The
two — the Christian Church of the past nineteen centuries, and the
vibrant, communal life of the churches in the first century — are
irreconcilable. ♣

---

[10] See James 2 and 5, as well as *The Insurgent* on page 21.   [11] Acts 6:1-7
[12] See *The Insurgent*, about the Epistle of James, on page 21.   [13] See *The Name
Above All Names* on page 151.   [14] These are found in First, Second, and Third
John as well as the letters to the churches in Revelation 2 and 3, and the letter of
James.

THE SPLENDOR OF... SMUT

Feeling adventurous? Pick up any fine dining magazine these days, and you are barraged with all manner of exotic foods to tantalize your taste buds. As Americans, we just don't seem to be satisfied with the "same ole, same ole" anymore. We're always looking for something new and exciting. Well lately, the rage has been none other than huitlacoche (pronounced, *wheat-la-CO-chay*). This South American delicacy has been popping up in all the upper-echelon restaurants. The rich, nutty flavor, sautéed with garlic, wild onions, and chives, set steaming on a bed of fresh, wild-crafted, mixed greens, has brought forth scrumptious reviews from food critics in all the major metro areas.

More commonly known to farmers as *corn smut*, this one-time nuisance to the agri-business has now become a big-time moneymaker for growers. In fact, many farmers have decided to *intentionally* inject the spores of this fungus into their crops to ensure they get the large, bluish, pustule-like masses that have become so *en vogue*. At a popular Madison, Wisconsin, farmers' market one infected ear will go for around $5.

So how is it that a disease that used to be so vigilantly fought against has become accepted and even sought-after? To the common man, this deformed, mushroom-like growth might seem repulsive. Poor fellow! While he may look on and scratch his head in amazement, blinded by his lack of culture, the trained palates of the intellectually astute will continue their chitter-chatter about the splendor of smut.

The Disease Cycle

Though the concept may sound strange, it's not the first time something obviously bad has later come to be seen as something desirable. One of the most profound examples of this phenomenon wasn't with a vegetable, but with the church. Although it began centuries ago, this odd transformation continues to this day.

So often, Yahshua used simple analogies from nature to communicate a deep message to His hearers. In fact, on numerous occasions, both He and the prophets compared Israel, and later the first-century church, to a plant.[1] Plants are dependent on the sun for growth and reproduction, and if the light is hindered from reaching them, fungi and decay set in.[2]

The first-century church began like a healthy and vibrant vine, bearing its fruit in clusters. You can read about it in the following verses:

> *All who believed were together and had all things in common. And they were selling their possessions and belongings and distributing the proceeds to all, as any had need...The full number of those who believed were of one heart and soul, and no one said that any of the things that belonged to him was his own, but they had everything in common. And with great power the apostles were giving their testimony to the resurrection of the Lord Jesus, and great grace was upon them all. There was not a needy person among them, for as many as were owners of lands or houses sold them and brought the proceeds of what was sold and laid it at the apostles' feet, and it was distributed to each as any had need. (Acts 2:44-45; 4:32-35)*

Like a healthy crop, the church started off full of the necessary nutrients and oriented properly toward the "Sun," from which all of its life came. Continued reliance upon the nutrients of the Master's commands and the apostles' teaching would ensure strong, healthy growth.[3] The fulfillment of the words of Yahshua[4] was coming about, for

---

[1] Ezekiel 17:22-24; Matthew 13:31-32 [2] See *The Colors of Life and Death*, page 3.
[3] Matthew 28:18-20; John 14:15 [4] See *The Name Above All Names* on page 151.

when asked by the Pharisees when the Kingdom of God was going to come, He answered:

> "... The kingdom of God is not coming with signs to be observed; nor will they say, 'Look, here it is!' or, 'There it is!' For behold, the kingdom of God is in your midst." (Luke 17:20-21)

The life of the Kingdom of God was in their midst in a comprehensive and observable way.[5] All of those who believed were *together* sharing all that they had, living in unity with one another, for they had been cleansed from their sins, and the love of God had been poured out into their hearts.[6] This was no accident. No, the prophets had spoken long ago of such a movement:

> This is what the Sovereign LORD says: "I myself will take a shoot from the very top of a cedar and plant it; I will break off a tender sprig from its topmost shoots and plant it on a high and lofty mountain. On the mountain heights of Israel I will plant it; it will produce branches and bear fruit and become a splendid cedar. Birds of every kind will nest in it; they will find shelter in the shade of its branches." (Ezekiel 17:22-23)

And Yahshua had echoed this when He said:

> "The kingdom of heaven is like a mustard seed, which a man took and planted in his field. Though it is the smallest of all your seeds, yet when it grows, it is the largest of garden plants and becomes a tree, so that the birds of the air come and perch in its branches." (Matthew 13:31-32)

Slowly, however, spores from other fields began to drift into the branches of this healthy tree and lodge themselves there. Though the apostles warned of this danger, those who tended the field let their guard down.[7] Foreign agents crept in unnoticed, injecting their deadly fungus into the once-pure tree. The Apostle Paul lamented this process of decay, using a different metaphor:

> I am jealous for you with a godly jealousy. I promised you to one husband, to Christ, so that I might present you as a pure virgin to him. But I am afraid that just as Eve was deceived by the serpent's cunning, your minds may somehow be led astray from your sincere and pure devotion to Christ. For if someone comes to you and preaches a Jesus other than the Jesus we preached, or if you receive a different spirit from the one you received, or a different gospel from the one you accepted, you put up with it easily enough... For such men are false apostles, deceitful workmen, masquerading as apostles of Christ. And no wonder, for Satan himself masquerades as an angel of light. It is not surprising, then, if his servants

---

[5] 1 Peter 2:12   [6] 1 Corinthians 1:10; 1 Timothy 2:8; Romans 5:5; John 17:21-23
[7] Galatians 1:6-7

*masquerade as servants of righteousness. Their end will be what their
actions deserve. (2 Corinthians 11:2-4,13-15)*

The true light of Messiah was being supplanted by the false light of
Satan's messengers, accelerating the cycle of decay that had already
lodged itself in some of the communities, perverting the healthy growth
the church had started out with.[8] With time, though, the alarms were
sounded less frequently. The original apostles started dying off, and *smut*
infected the entire crop. The church stopped obeying even the most
fundamental commands they had been taught. They stopped caring for
the orphans in their midst, nor did they make sure the widows had what
they needed, nor did they welcome strangers. A deadly fungus had
gripped this once-majestic tree and was starting to transform it into
something completely different from what it had been in the beginning.

A man named James, writing early in the second century AD,
penned a desperate plea to the churches, which by that time had already
become divided and dispersed all over the known world.[9] He hoped that
perhaps, through his earnest pleas, he could somehow get the attention of
any true disciples that might be left. We still have his letter today. Here is
a part of it, showing the decayed condition of the church:

> *If anyone among you thinks he is religious, and does not bridle his tongue
> but deceives his own heart, this one's religion is useless. Pure and undefiled
> religion before God and the Father is this: to visit orphans and widows in
> their trouble, and to keep oneself unspotted from the world...*
>
> *My brethren, do not hold the faith of our Lord Jesus Christ, the Lord of
> glory, with partiality. For if there should come into your assembly a man
> with gold rings, in fine apparel, and there should also come in a poor man
> in filthy clothes, and you pay attention to the one wearing the fine clothes
> and say to him, "You sit here in a good place," and say to the poor man,
> "You stand there," or, "Sit here at my footstool," have you not shown
> partiality among yourselves, and become judges with evil thoughts? ...*
>
> *What does it profit, my brethren, if someone says he has faith but does not
> have works? Can faith save him? If a brother or sister is naked and
> destitute of daily food, and one of you says to them, "Depart in peace, be
> warmed and filled," but you do not give them the things which are needed
> for the body, what does it profit? Thus also faith by itself, if it does not
> have works, is dead. But someone will say, "You have faith, and I have
> works." Show me your faith without your works, and I will show you my*

---

[8] Isaiah 50:11 [9] James 1:1 — This is not to be confused with the brother of
Christ, or even James the apostle, since this letter was written during the second
century AD. Though many Christian scholars believe that the letter was written
around 40-45 AD, it would have been impossible for the communities to have
fallen that far in such a short amount of time. See *The Insurgent* on page 21.

faith by my works. You believe that there is one God. You do well. Even the demons believe — and tremble! ... But do you want to know, O foolish man, that faith without works is dead? For as the body without the spirit is dead, so faith without works is dead also." (James 1:26-27; 2:1-4,14-19,26)

The *smut* had set in and was now beginning to take over.

A Modern-Day Delicacy

Sadly, the passionate appeals of James were not enough to arrest the disease that was spreading lethally throughout the entire church.

normal kernel   *smut-infected kernel*

The pustules of division grew into councils, factions, and denominations that multiplied and mutated into varied malformations. The spores spread from one city to the next, and down through the centuries, infecting entire nations of people and almost exterminating others.

Though many people over the centuries lamented the destruction of this once-pure growth, others in more learned and scholarly circles came to appreciate the variety of newer forms, and even began celebrating the mystical oneness of the many-splintered diversity as if it were a delicacy. Like corn smut, this new growth was heralded by the theologically elite as a better, more glorious and mature form than the simple common life of love and unity described so vividly in the book of Acts.

So, today we find ourselves living in a society that values things like *huitlacoche*, which is really a lifeless fungus, void of any nutritional value. Sadly, like this fungus, many take delight in the lifeless husk of a religion that has grown accustomed to the things that James so aggressively warned against. Though most will read this and find little wrong with a religion that boasts 39,000 denominations worldwide, there will be a few (perhaps you are one of them) in whom it will awaken a longing for something real, something that gives life and doesn't leech it away.

It is for those few that we write, in hopes that something will stir in their hearts, for we have found the One who satisfies and doesn't disappoint. While much of the world is being dazzled by the flashy façades of Christianity, there is a little sprout bursting forth from the "mustard seed" to spread its branches and make a home for those who desire life. ❦

A father of the fatherless and a judge for widows is God in His holy habitation. God makes a home for the lonely; He leads out the prisoners into prosperity; Only the rebellious dwell in a parched land. (Psalm 68:5-6)

THE INSURGENT

THE FIRST RADICAL PAMPHLET IN CHRISTIAN HISTORY AND WHY MARTIN LUTHER REVILED IT

They call it the Epistle of James. It is found near the end of the New Testament. Tradition says the author was "the brother of the Lord" and that he wrote it to the Jews living outside Judea. Most scholars date it within 30 years of the founding of the Church. Many say it was written as early as 45 AD. Tradition is a powerful force, isn't it? It often carries more influence than common sense. If you are one who places more weight on tradition than on common sense, don't bother reading this article. But if you consider yourself a free thinker, then please consider this as well:

Most assumptions about the Book of James are wrong. They are neither based on the letter itself nor on hard historical evidence. And worst of all, these fallacies aren't just the result of ignorance — they are attempts to deny and conceal a dirty little secret. But we'll discuss that later. First, let's consider the objective evidence.

Who Wrote It and When

The author only refers to himself as "James, a bondservant of God and of the Lord Jesus Christ." Beyond this, he makes no reference to his own identity, or authority, or place of residence, as Paul, Peter, and John do in their letters. Christian tradition presumes him to be "the brother of

the Lord" based simply on another presumption of Christian tradition —
that everything in the New Testament must have been written by an
apostle or a bishop or somebody important in the clergy. And Christian
tradition further presumes that the clergy-laity system was part of the
foundation of the early Church.

Of course, we can tell from what Paul wrote that a distinction
between clergy and laity was foreign to the early Church.[1] According to
Paul, all disciples were expected to take their identity as priests seriously
and to bring to each gathering a song, a teaching, a revelation, and so on,
and he encouraged all the disciples to prophesy. This is supported by
Hebrews 3:6, which tells us that the defining characteristic of God's
house is something translated as "confidence" — the *parrhesia* (literally
"outspokenness" or "freedom of speech") of the people.

So there is no reason, other than the traditions of the clergy-laity
system, to think of the writer James as being an apostle or even a leader in
the early Church. There is every reason to believe that, like many of the
Old Testament prophets, he rose from obscurity, moved by the Holy
Spirit to express his concerns.

The usual date assigned to the writing (45-63 AD) is also a
presumption, based on the presumption that James, "the Lord's brother"
(who is supposed to have been killed around 63 AD), is the author. Some
scholars have objected to an early date, arguing that the spiritual
condition James addresses is such a stark contrast with the fervor of the
disciples at the time of Pentecost. Others reason that the sins he
mentions "could have been found in the Church at any decade of its
history" — a remarkable rationalization which we will address shortly.
First, though, let's consider who received this "epistle."

Who It Was Written To

The opening sentence says, "to the twelve tribes scattered abroad."
The traditional take on this phrase is that "the Lord's brother" wrote a
general letter to all the Jews who lived outside of Judea — as if they
would have read a letter from someone in a despised sect that was spoken
against everywhere.[2] But there is a problem with presuming that these
"twelve tribes" are the physical tribes of Israel. You see, only the two
tribes of the Babylonian captivity, Judah and Benjamin, along with a few
Levites, retained any identity as Israelites. The other ten tribes, taken
captive by Assyria, had been swallowed up by the surrounding cultures,
and it would have been impossible to address a letter to them. Besides,
the term "twelve tribes" would hardly refer to the Jews (technically, only
one tribe), and could scarcely be applied to Jewish believers (comprising
only a small percentage of that tribe).

---

[1] 1 Corinthians 14:26-32   [2] Acts 28:22

Actually, other references in the New Testament make it clear that the term "twelve tribes" referred to the whole Church — a spiritual nation made up of both physical Jews and physical Gentiles. For example, the "Bride of Christ" in Revelation is pictured as a city with twelve gates, each gate being one of the twelve tribes of Israel.[3] Also, in Paul's trial before King Agrippa[4] he said that, in order to attain the promise made to Abraham, the "twelve tribes" that Paul was part of were earnestly serving God night and day — and this was why the Jews (obviously not part of the tribes he referred to) were accusing him.

Given the objective evidence, it is clear that the "twelve tribes" James was writing to was identical with the "Commonwealth of Israel" of Ephesians 2:12, made up of both Jews and Gentiles, who had been made into one nation by the blood of Messiah. But there were some problems in the commonwealth, and that is what moved James to write.

Why He Wrote It

James saw that the new nation — the one Messiah had purchased with the sacrifice of His own life[5] — was on the verge of being destroyed. Those who had been united through the cleansing power of His blood were now becoming alienated from one another, because His blood was no longer covering their sins. And the reason their sins were not being covered was that they were no longer confessing and forsaking their sins.[6] The Church was in deep trouble — and it wasn't just one or two communities, such as Corinth or Laodicea, it was the whole nation (the twelve tribes). There was a shocking contrast between the condition of the Church that James was writing to and the quality of the life the disciples lived at the time of Pentecost.

Unlike the congregation described in Acts 4:32, who were all of "one heart and soul," James portrayed a Church that was splintered by quarrels and conflicts, largely as a result of the poor members envying the rich.[7] That envy was based in part on the failure of the prosperous to meet the needs of the less prosperous,[8] but both the envy of the poor and the self-centeredness of the rich could be traced to friendship with and love for the world,[9] which James flatly condemned as spiritual adultery. Not only

---

[3] Revelation 21:9-12 [4] Acts 26:6-7 [5] Revelation 5:9-10 [6] 1 John 1:9; Proverbs 28:13 [7] James 4:1-3 [8] James 2:14-17 [9] James 4:4

were the prosperous neglecting the needs of others, but the poor were being slighted socially, while the rich were lavished with attention. James rebuked this practice as inconsistent with having faith in Messiah.[10]

Despite the sins of the affluent, James did not justify those who were envious of them. He condemned both bitter jealousy and selfish ambition as demonic,[11] especially when those attitudes resulted in defaming their fellow disciples.[12] To those who would not bridle their tongue, but hypocritically blessed God while cursing men made in His image, James declared their religion to be worthless.[13] Still, he reserved his harshest words for those who stored up riches, especially by unjust means:

Now listen, you rich people, weep and wail because of the misery that is coming upon you. Your wealth has rotted, and moths have eaten your clothes. Your gold and silver are corroded. Their corrosion will testify against you and eat your flesh like fire. You have hoarded wealth in the last days… (James 5:1-5)

The topic that James is best remembered for, however, is that of faith versus works. But it wasn't just a general doctrinal subject that he addressed with theological detachment. He was specifically attacking the lack of love in the Church that spawned their favoritism toward the rich and neglect of the needy.[14] He was alarmed to find so rare those *works of love* which had been so common in the Church's infancy. He was appalled at the complacency of those who failed to meet their brother's needs while still professing to have faith.[15] He even boldly challenged their claim of being saved.[16] So-called faith, without *works of love*, was to James not only useless,[17] but also dead.[18]

The scenario painted by James is so vastly different from the portrait of the Church in the book of Acts that it leads the reader to wonder whether the two writings were actually talking about the same group. In Acts, the brethren were devoted to the teachings of the apostles, were together, associated with each other, were of one mind, one heart, and one soul, gladly ate their meals together, shared everything they had, and even sold their possessions to meet the needs of their brothers, to the point that none among them were needy.[19] In James, however, the

---

[10] James 2:1-13 [11] James 3:14-16 [12] James 4:11; 5:9 [13] James 1:26; 3:8-12
[14] James 2:8-10 [15] James 2:19-20 [16] James 2:14-17 [17] James 2:20
[18] James 2:17,26 [19] Acts 2:42-46; 4:32-35

brethren heard the apostles' teaching but did not do it,[20] were continually traveling from town to town in search of financial gain,[21] were divided along economic lines,[22] and even defamed and quarreled with each other because of the economic injustice in their midst.[23]

The Church that James was writing to had degenerated far beyond the condition of the individual churches addressed elsewhere in the New Testament. Paul's letters to the Corinthians (written around 55 AD) spoke of the foolishness and carnality of an immature community, but gave clear direction what they must do in order to grow up. John's letters to the churches in the book of Revelation (written around 90 AD) pointed out the things each one was faithful in, as well as the things they had fallen away from, and once again, called each church to heed the specific warnings and mend its ways or else face the consequences. James, however, was writing unilaterally to all the churches, addressing a spiritual condition virtually identical to that of the Pharisaical Judaism the Son of God had called His followers out from. For the Church to have reached that state, James could not have been writing before the beginning of the second century AD.

General Epistle or Underground Tract?

Unlike the writings of Paul and John, which gave authoritative direction to specific churches, James only stated the general problems and made an appeal to *individual* disciples to obey the commandments of their Master if they found themselves in those situations. It is as if James had no hope of calling the Church back to the *deeds of love* that characterized the Church at Pentecost. John, on the other hand, specifically commanded the Ephesians[24] to repent and do the *deeds of love* they had done in the beginning, for if they did not, their lampstand (their validity before God as a church) would be taken away. But James did not try to keep any lampstands lit. Things had degenerated beyond that point, and all he could do was simply warn the *rich men*[25] in the congregations (he did not refer to them as *brothers*) about the judgment coming upon them and appeal to each of the *brothers*[26] who were oppressed by them to bear their sufferings patiently and be true to the commands of the Master.

It is obvious from the context that the sins James was confronting had become accepted practices within the Church. It made him so distraught that he wrote down the burden of his heart and began distributing the document to the entire Church. And so, rather than being a "general epistle" by someone in authority, the "Epistle of James" is clearly more of an "under-ground manuscript" exposing the problems that the shepherds and elders and overseers had turned a blind eye to. James

---

[20] James 1:22; 4:17   [21] James 4:13   [22] James 2:2-4   [23] James 4:1 - 5:9
[24] Revelation 2:4-5   [25] James 1:10   [26] James 1:9

himself, rather than holding the prestigious position of "the Lord's brother," was more of an insurgent — not outwardly belligerent against the hierarchy of the compromising Church, but inwardly revolting against their accepted policies. It's not hard to imagine the outrage among the rich and prosperous which this little essay generated originally — back when it wasn't tucked away in the back of the Bible and watered down by commentaries. Just think what would happen if you stood up in the midst of a worship service and read aloud his condemnation of the rich.[27]

Why They Got It Wrong

Someone may ask, "So if James was really an obscure outsider in the second century, grieved by sins the Church was tolerating, why don't most people see it that way, and how did his writings become part of the Bible?" The second question is the simplest to answer: James is part of the Bible because it is almost entirely a restatement of Messiah's teachings. It had to become part of the canon because it is so utterly orthodox. The first question takes a little more explanation.

Recall that some commentators claimed that the sins James spoke of "could have been found in the Church at any decade of its history." There was a reason for that rationalization: To admit that backbiting, defamation, favoritism, quarrels, and (most of all) divisions between rich and poor were not part of the status quo in the first century Church would raise a very uncomfortable question: "Why have they been the status quo throughout the rest of Christian history?"

It is very convenient, even comforting, to claim that James was "the Lord's brother" writing in 45 AD. That would mean that the obvious deeds of the flesh[28] were running rampant through the Church scarcely a decade after it was founded. And if the Lord's brother could do no more about it than moan weakly, "these things ought not to be this way," then that lets the rest of us off the hook, doesn't it? If this is the way it has always been, then this is the way it will always be, because the flesh is just too strong and human nature is too warped to do anything about it. The

---

[27] James 5:1-3   [28] Galatians 5:19-21

obvious conclusion: "All we can do is just have faith in the Lord and wait 'til we get to heaven."

Most people are content to accept such rationalizations and cover up the "dirty little secret" that the whole Church fell away from the faith around the end of the first century. Most people miss the fact that James tells us twice[29] that "faith" without works is dead, once that such "faith" is useless,[30] and once that such "faith" cannot save a person.[31] They eagerly agree with him that "no man can tame the tongue,"[32] but overlook his comment that if a man does not bridle his tongue,[33] then his religion is completely worthless. But not all people are quite that dull. Martin Luther wasn't. What James said about bridling the tongue irked him, because Luther was never one to control his tongue. What James said about works being the proof of faith especially irked Luther, because it messed up his pet theory that "faith alone" was all God required. That is why Luther called James an "epistle of straw."

Hopefully, you who read this will be as perceptive as Luther, but rather than rejecting what James had to say about works, you will understand the implications of it. Consider what happened to the false "faith" that had taken over the Church in James' day and failed to produce the works of love that were normal for all disciples when the Church began. Did it go away? Was it replaced by a resurgence of the self-denying love that motivated the believers at Pentecost? Hasn't the bad fruit of that "faith" only gotten worse over the last nineteen centuries, in spite of reformations and counter-reformations and countless so-called revivals? Instead, isn't it time for the restoration of the life of love that resulted from the message of the apostles? The "faith" that has been passed down to us by organized religion is none other than the false "faith" James was exposing — a "faith" that cannot save. Only if we can realize this do we have any hope of being delivered from a worthless religion where such "faith" is the norm and brought back to the true faith that turned the world upside down.[34] ❧

---

[29] James 2:17,26   [30] James 2:20   [31] James 2:14   [32] James 3:8   [33] James 1:26
[34] Acts 17:6

THE TIME BETWEEN THE LIGHTS

Twilight is the time between the lights. The bright light of the sun is fading, and the shadowy light of the moon and the stars is taking its place. Night is coming. It's dusky then, when shapes and dangers are indistinct. In the early church, it was the time of transition from the fervor of the first days, as seen in the community in Jerusalem described in Acts 2 and 4, to the complacency and worldliness a generation later.

A "good" example of this is the Corinthian church. In his first letter to them, Paul addressed very serious problems, grave lacks of wisdom, and a shameful example of immorality such as would make even the Greek world of that day blush. But at least he had the confidence to deal with the problems in the belief that somehow they still had the same Lord.[1]

By the time he wrote his second letter to them, he wrote in fear and trembling that they may have already been deceived by the Serpent of old, the devil. His ministers among them masqueraded their true nature and real intentions so well that Paul called them "super apostles."[2] His words to the Corinthians were full of irony concerning how well they bore deception and even received another spirit:

> For if one comes and preaches another Jesus whom we have not preached, or you receive a different spirit which you have not received, or a different

---

[1] The Corinthians were worldly and carnal (1 Corinthians 3). There were serious questions whether anyone with wisdom lived in that community (1 Corinthians 6). They had ceased sharing their meals together with gladness and sincerity of heart as the believers had in Jerusalem (1 Corinthians 11 and Acts 2:42). Because of their easy toleration of sin, many among them had become sick and died (1 Corinthians 11:30). They even tolerated gross immorality (1 Corinthians 5).

[2] 2 Corinthians 11:2-15

29

gospel which you have not accepted, you bear this beautifully. (2 Corinthians 11:4)

This did not happen all at once, but the light of Messiah, which was His love dwelling in a people who loved as He loved,[3] was fading fast. The signs were everywhere for those who had eyes to see, and were recorded for our benefit so that we would not be deceived in the same manner. Another "light" was filling the church. The Savior had already spoken of this light in Matthew 6:

> *But if your eye is bad, your whole body will be full of darkness. If therefore the light that is in you is darkness, how great is that darkness! No one can serve two masters; for either he will hate the one and love the other, or else he will be loyal to the one and despise the other. You cannot serve God and mammon. (Matthew 6:23-24)*

Despising the Savior began in personal compromise; "little" things crept in so subtly and slowly that it was hard to see what was happening. In comparison to the gross sins of the world, things like failing to confess their sins, neglecting their children, and resisting their leaders were not very noticeable. In time, however, these things would lead to outright challenges to even the apostles' authority.[4] They would end up enthusiastically serving *mammon*. But right away it led to something not so obvious — the loss of spiritual confidence on the part of many.

This led to the loss of their outspokenness in the assembly, where once all were speaking and all were prophesying.[5] They had once lived in the reality of what would later be called the "priesthood of all believers" where each one had the freedom and the grace to help the other, to speak in the gatherings, to evangelize, and even to prophesy. That priesthood was fading away in the face of the little acts of compromise and cowardice. In its place, another more exclusive priesthood was arising. These were the Nicolaitans,[6] the men who presumed to speak for everyone. They made it increasingly clear that no longer was everyone welcomed to speak up and share their revelations and their concerns.

Without this confidence to speak, however, an event of great, even cosmic significance took place. *Cosmic* means pertaining to the entire universe, inconceivably extending in space or time. Yet, it passed very quietly and was largely unnoticed except by the sensitive few.

Messiah ceased to be the head over their house.

This happened one community at a time, as the infection spread, until the lampstands[7] — the light of revelation from the Father — were extinguished in the entire church:

---

[3] John 13:34-35 [4] 1 Corinthians 9; 2 Corinthians 11:5 - 12:1 [5] 1 Corinthians 14:1-3,23-32 [6] The term *Nicolaitan* is derived from *nikao*, "to conquer," and *laos*, "people," hence, "people conquerors." The Nicolaitan movement marks the beginning of the separation of people into clergy and laity. [7] Revelation 2:5

But Christ as a son over his own house; whose house are we, if we hold fast the confidence and the rejoicing of the hope firm unto the end. (Hebrews 3:6)

The word translated *confidence* meant what they no longer had – "freedom in speaking, unreservedness in speech, open, frank, free and fearless confidence."[8] At the same time, the sheep were being beaten down and oppressed by self-seeking shepherds, as the Master had warned would come.[9] Paul said that after his departure, "savage wolves" would arise among the leaders, leading a following after themselves. Both of these prophetic warnings were fulfilled by men like Diotrephes, in 3 John,

I wrote to the church, but Diotrephes, who loves to have the preeminence among them, does not receive us. Therefore, if I come, I will call to mind his deeds which he does, prating against us with malicious words. And not content with that, he himself does not receive the brethren, and forbids those who wish to, putting them out of the church. (3 John 1:9-10)

What would these proud men, so bold as to speak maliciously against the *apostles*, say to the sheep? But the destructive, intimidating, and silencing effect of their words we don't have to imagine, for history records the silence that soon settled upon the churches. It was settled practice by 150 AD.[10] Soon the speakers needed special garments to set them off from the common people. Naturally, they chose not the Biblical sign of purity and a good conscience — white robes — but just the opposite.

The Outward Sign

Outward signs are used for many reasons: to point the way, to warn, even to mock. In the Scriptures, white garments are the clothing of the Bride of Messiah and a figurative sign of individual purity.

---

[8] *Confidence* is #3954 in the Greek Concordance.   [9] Luke 12:45
[10] Earle E. Cairns writes in *Christianity through the Centuries* (Zondervan Publishing House, Grand Rapids, Michigan), p. 83, that as early as the middle of the second century, worship consisted not of the spontaneous overflow Paul describes in 1 Corinthians 14, but of several *readings* from epistles and the prophets, a *homily* by the "president," responsorial prayer by the people [they said "Amen" on cue], the Lord's supper, and collection of the offering, which was followed by dismissal of the people to their homes. And so it is to this day. The people were silenced.

"Let us be glad and rejoice and give Him glory, for the marriage of the Lamb has come, and His wife has made herself ready." To her it was granted to be arrayed in fine linen, clean and bright, for the fine linen is the righteous acts of the saints. (Revelation 19:7-8)

You have a few names even in Sardis who have not defiled their garments; and they shall walk with Me in white, for they are worthy. He who overcomes shall be clothed in white garments... (Revelation 3:4-5)

Stained or defiled garments are just the opposite of white garments, being a sign of a bad conscience. They represent unconfessed sin. Seen in this light, it is not a little surprising that the ancient garments of the clergy — allegedly the godly, spiritual leaders of the congregations — are black. It is just like a neglected conscience that accumulates guilt, becomes stained, and in the end is evil. An evil conscience has reached the point where good can be called evil, and evil good.

The black garments of the clergy (the Nicolaitans) were the outward sign, if anyone cared to notice it, of the evil they represented. It was more than mockery of the good conscience the shepherds were to have in taking care of the flock.[11] They were commanded by their Savior to be servants, but soon they became tyrannical monarchs. History even terms them *monarchal bishops*. And it is not only the Catholic Church that is *still* organized according to this pattern. In the beginning, they were men who arose from among the elders — as Paul warned would happen[12] — to take the prominent, leading role in each church. Eventually, these men behaved like the lords of the Gentiles, mocking, by their earthly power and authority, the very words of the Savior:

"You know that those who are considered rulers over the Gentiles lord it over them, and their great ones exercise authority over them. Yet it shall not be so among you; but whoever desires to become great among you shall be your servant. And whoever of you desires to be first shall be slave of all. For even the Son of Man did not come to be served, but to serve, and to give His life a ransom for many." (Mark 10:42-45)

So the light among them became darkness, and how great was that darkness! 🌿

---

[11] 1 Peter 5:2-3   [12] Acts 20:29-30

NIGHTFALL

Finally, the life of Messiah, whose life was the light of men, could no longer be found. The last of the overcomers died or were put out of the churches by men like Diotrephes,[1] who forcefully suppressed any perceived threat to their solitary authority, or interruptions to their windy monologues (called sermons today). Unlike the sun, which is promised to shine as long as the earth endures,[2] the light of revelation was only given to the humble, the ones willing to do His will. Such was Peter when he proclaimed Yahshua to be the Messiah, the Son of the living God.[3] Such men and women were the only ones with the life of the Son.[4] Darkness spread over the land as the last lampstands were taken out of their places,[5] when each church could no longer make the confession of 1 John 4:2. This meant, as the King James Version accurately puts it, that fewer and fewer churches could honestly say that Yahshua was incarnate in their midst. "Hereby know ye the Spirit of God: Every spirit that confesseth that Jesus Christ is come in the flesh is of God."

It was not a doctrinal issue that caused John to write the letter called "1 John" to the churches. It was a deeper issue regarding the people's rejection of their Savior. He was no longer welcome in their midst. His words were given lip service, but the people's hearts were far from Him. They were drifting further and further from the amazing life the early communities had, which was described at length in Acts 2 and 4. This love in action, made possible by His grace, was the faith, or persuasion,[6] that Jude had exhorted them to contend for in his letter.[7] He was not speaking of a collection of doctrines about what it meant to believe.

This was just what the Master warned the Ephesians was coming upon them in[8] if they did not do the deeds they had done at first. Tragically, this warning came just forty years after Paul had admonished this same church to love Messiah with an undying, incorruptible love.[9]

When the communities ceased to be the very incarnation of Messiah, then the darkness Yahshua predicted in John 9 fell on the earth:

---

[1] 3 John 1:9-10 [2] Genesis 8:22 [3] Matthew 16:15-17; John 7:17 [4] 1 John 5:12
[5] Revelation 2:5 [6] The Greek word translated as *faith* is *pistis*, which comes from *peitho*, meaning to persuade. [7] Jude 1:3 [8] Revelation 2:4-5 [9] Ephesians 6:24

I must work the works of Him who sent Me while it is day; the night is coming when no one can work. As long as I am in the world, I am the light of the world. (John 9:4-5)

Night fell as the church changed her very nature, a change seen intellectually in defining faith not as the persuasion of the Holy Spirit to do the will of the Father, but instead as the acceptance of a set of beliefs. This detachment of belief from the heart only mirrored the detachment of believers' lives from one another. The many sayings of Yahshua and His apostles to love in deed and truth, to abstain from the lusts of the world, to turn their backs on riches, power, and earthly comfort, lost all power to command. The love of Messiah compelled no one to actually obey His words,[10] proving that those who claimed to love Him lied — first to themselves, and then to the world.[11]

So the darkness Messiah prophesied of in John 9 only deepened and darkened as the spores of this lethal new belief spread from church to church. Eventually, she indulged in cruel ill-treatment of all who questioned or doubted her. This lifeless belief and cruelty spread over all the earth and down many centuries of time. It was the exact opposite of the witness of the Kingdom that Messiah prophesied would one day be seen by the whole world.[12] In spite of rivers of words to the contrary, this false gospel had no power to release anyone from his contract with sin and death, which held sway over the whole world as soon as night fell.

Thereafter, the only "light" people could relate to as they read their Bibles longingly, wonderingly, was the light of the sun in the sky, and the fruitfulness of the fields on the earth below, to remind them of the time when another light was shining. The willing hearts of those men, gathered in communities, had been like God's fruitful gardens, bearing the fruit of the Spirit. Yet soon, it was only ancient history, hidden in the past, untouchable in the present.

Still, as the lives of the apostles and first disciples became the stuff of legend, the simple stories and profound parables of the Savior about farming, fishing, baking, and treasures hidden in fields, lived on. Those words continued to fill men with hope. Perhaps the day would come again when that same light would dawn on the earth, breaking the terrible spiritual darkness covering the world after the death of the early church. It had been smothered in a potent mass of spiritual infection and disease, like so much smut feeding on the memory and the very words of that Savior and His apostles, just as the parasitic fungus called *smut* feeds on corn. Like that dark fungus, the men in their soiled, stained garments — the black robes of the clergy — spread an entirely different life from the one found in the true seed of the Word. ❧

---

[10] 2 Corinthians 5:14-15 [11] John 14:24 [12] Matthew 24:14

THE FAVORED RELIGION

Most Christians today have no idea that the basic tenets of their faith, religious practice, and doctrine come from the *integration of the church and the state*[1] during the reign of the Roman Emperor Constantine. That may not initially seem so alarming, but actually it has had a very significant effect on what Christians have believed down through history, and how they have lived, even to the present day. Although Christians would universally say they are taught from the words of Christ himself, the effect of those words is radically different than it was two thousands years ago. The gospels and epistles have been carefully preserved, yes, but their influence, interpretation, and application stem *not* from the pattern of the first-century church, but from the writings and councils of the early "church fathers" of the third and fourth centuries. It was a time when the church was in its last phase of *transition* into its current form.[2]

Contending for "The Faith"

For nearly two centuries the church had experienced a steady decline from its original vibrancy of living together *in community*, when love was the glue which held their life together.[3] That love, resulting in the real unity of "having all things in common,"[4] was the fruit of the gospel first preached by the apostles. Yet the book of Jude already records, near the end of the first century, the writer's alarm and distress, as Jude pleads with all the churches to contend earnestly for "the faith" that was delivered to them once for all by the apostles themselves.

That term "once for all" means there was no other foundation upon which a valid church could be established.[5] "The faith" delivered to them by the apostles was their spiritual foundation, the result of the gospel they had received. It was expressed through the visible and tangible life they shared together, having a community of goods. This was the outward expression of their "obedience from the heart"[6] to the good news of salvation they had received.[7]

---

[1] The *Edict of Milan*, early in 313.   [2] *Transition* — a process or period in which something undergoes a change from one state, form, or activity to another.
[3] John 13:34-35   [4] Acts 2:44 and 4:32   [5] 1 Corinthians 3:9-11; Ephesians 2:20-22; 1 Corinthians 12:12   [6] Romans 6:17   [7] They had embraced the terms of peace in Luke 14:31-32 and made peace with the coming king, Luke 14:33.

Jude describes it as their "common salvation" which all the churches universally held, having been established by the apostles. These men, God's special ambassadors,[8] were supremely loyal to their Savior. Jude 1:4 tells how *that life* was threatened, challenged, and ultimately destroyed by apostates. An apostate is one who has departed from being devoted to the fellowship of the original apostles and their teachings, while, deceptively, maintaining a pretense of it.[9] Peter himself says these apostate "brothers" were the very ones perverting the gospel. In the end, as the apostles testified, it would result in their destruction, according to their deeds.[10]

> *For certain men have crept in unnoticed, who long ago were marked out for this condemnation, ungodly men, who turn the grace of our God into a license for immorality and deny our only Master and Lord Jesus Christ... These are grumblers, complainers, walking according to their own lusts; and they mouth great swelling words, flattering people to gain advantage."* (Jude 1:4,16)

The second letter to the Corinthians also speaks of Paul's alarm over the imminent loss of the original simplicity and purity of "the faith" he had passed on to them. Through craft and scheming the apostates twisted the scriptures, even the very gospel of the Lord, delivered through the apostles. They rejected the authority of the apostles and sought to promote themselves as those who are first among their brothers.[11]

> *For if he who comes preaches another Jesus whom we have not preached, or if you receive a different spirit which you have not received, or a different gospel which you have not accepted, you bear this beautifully!... For such men are false apostles, deceitful workers, transforming themselves into apostles of Christ. And no wonder! For even Satan transforms himself into an angel of light. Therefore, it is no surprise if his ministers also transform themselves into ministers of righteousness, whose end will be according to their works.* (2 Corinthians 11:4,13-15)

There is a consistency in the writings of the apostles in the way these treacherous apostates (self-proclaimed apostles) are described. They held to a form of godliness, but did not have revelation or power from the Holy Spirit. They were natural men, not spiritual, and like brute beasts they ravaged the sheep, causing confusion and division within the church and its leadership.[12] They knew well the hardships of the churches in every place and played upon this very fact to captivate a receptive audience.

Subtly, these false ministers gained an advantage, motivated by selfish desires, not seeking the welfare of the sheep or its fold, but only to promote themselves, their own name, for their own glory.[13] With self-

---

[8] 2 Corinthians 5:18-20 [9] 1 John 1:3; 2:19,20,27; Jude 1:17-19 [10] 2 Peter 2:1-3,19; 3:16; 2 Corinthians 11:15; 1 John 1:3; 2:19 [11] 2 Peter 2:10; Jude 1:8; 3 John 1:9-10 [12] Acts 20:28-30 [13] John 7:17-18; Jude 1:8,12,13,17-19

sacrificing love no longer being the standard by which a true believer's confession of faith could be judged, another standard had to be found. So it was no wonder these "deceitful workers"[14] were able, through their speech and persuasion, to captivate the mind and intellect of the fallen church remnant. Community was no longer the "litmus test" by which the authenticity of their faith could be judged, but *doctrine* was hailed as the standard to determine whether one "believed." Their gospel required nothing more than mental assent, producing a dead religion of "belief" only. Hence, by the end of the third century, the church was splintered by bickering bishops and a docile laity, ready for a new era.

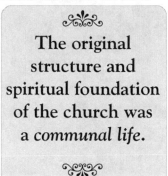

The original structure and spiritual foundation of the church was a *communal life.*

The Fatal Transition: Emperor Constantine

According to some scholars, this new era brought the completion of a *fatal transition* from which the church would never again recover its original Judean pattern.[15] Community, which had long ago dissolved,[16] was the only means by which those first disciples had shared a "common salvation." Its original structure and spiritual foundation was a *communal life*, yet by the fourth century the church had become entirely different in nature from the original pattern that is explicit in Acts 2:41-47 and 4:32-37, and assumed throughout the epistles.[17]

After a lengthy period of persecution, spiritual decline, and constant friction from within, Constantine baited the already-weakened ranks of the church. The Roman world during the second and third centuries had long been divided by the continual unrest of civil war, foreign invasion, and disorder of every sort. Constantine sought a means to unify the crumbling empire. At the same time, the churches of the western and eastern provinces suffered tremendously under the strain of both the Empire and the constant influence of apostates. Over two hundred years of factions from within and persecutions from without held the church continually in the place of compromise and hypocrisy.

---

[14] 2 Corinthians 11:13 [15] "Between the years AD 100 and AD 500 the Christian Church changed almost beyond recognition. [At first] the organization of the church was still fluid... there were no creeds to be recited, no set forms of worship... [By AD 500] the worship of the church was entirely liturgical with fixed, set forms of prayer." (Tony Lane, *The Lion Book of Christian Thought*, Lion Publishing Company, Batavia, Illinois, 1984, p. 8) [16] Dissolve — 1) to fade away gradually and disappear, or make something gradually fade away and disappear; 2) to break up, or break something up, into smaller or more basic parts; 3) to bring a legal relationship, for example, a business partnership or a marriage, formally to an end. [17] 1 Thessalonians 2:14

Early in the fourth century, Constantine resolved to protect himself and his own provinces against the threat of other challenging Roman rulers and marauders who contended for control of the weakened empire. He went to war against Maxentius in order to secure his territories. The account of Bishop Eusebius, an ardent admirer of Constantine and a devout Christian, says that as Constantine approached Rome he was given a vision to conquer under the sign of the Cross. He had this emblem affixed to the shields of his soldiers (most of whom were pagans) as they went into battle. Far outnumbered by Maxentius' army, Constantine won a decisive victory. From then on, he worked tirelessly to unite the fractured church and bring it into intimate fellowship with the Roman state. This merger of church and state set the stage for Christianity's development over the next 1700 years.

Constantine's Maneuver

Seizing the opportunity, Constantine maneuvered the church and its leaders through flattery, luring them into an inescapable relationship with that of the state. Eusebius proudly notes Constantine's gifts of money, property, and a massive church building program as the blessing of God to His once-struggling, persecuted church.[18] Publicly acknowledging the Christian God for the victory gained, Constantine believed this same God would now protect the Roman Empire from harm as long as the emperors worshiped Him and the church remained both united and devoted to the Empire. Sniffing the hope of an end to persecution and a path to prosperity, the leaders of the fourth-century church swallowed the bait, hook, line, and sinker.

Constantine called a series of church councils to bring unity among the bickering bishops. He didn't simply command them to come; he paid their expenses and even provided their means of getting there. Then, while still holding his position as the head of the state pagan religion,

---

[18] Eusebius, *The Church History of Eusebius*, Book X, Chapters VI and VII. As the Encarta 2000 article on Constantine puts it: "He gave huge estates and other gifts to the Christian church." And he did none of this, it should be noted, without expecting an ample return of loyalty and obedience on his investment.

Constantine presided over the councils and enforced their decisions. These councils and the creeds that came forth from them are held in the highest regard in Christianity. They formed the basis of identifying what is and what is not Christian faith, practice, and doctrine ever since. From then on, they have been the foundation for all orthodox Christian faith and practice, both of which are far different from the life of the apostolic churches as recorded in the New Testament.[19]

After nearly three centuries of struggle, the walls between the church and the world came tumbling down,[20] completing its transformation.[21] Constantine promoted Christians to positions of prominence within the state and surrounded himself with Christian advisers. He exempted the clergy from the heavy and difficult duties of Roman citizenship.[22] After all, ethically and morally speaking, the Christians' code of living raised the standard of Roman society. Before long Constantine even had Christian bishops accompany his troops into battle to ensure God's favor and to strengthen the moral character of his armies. He built magnificent cathedrals and Roman buildings in honor of the Christian God and began paying salaries out of the state treasury to church leaders. He passed laws in favor of the church in exchange for obligatory state service.[23] He

---

[19] This exactly parallels the training of lawyers today in constitutional law. They are not taught the Constitution, but rather, the judicial interpretations of it, especially Supreme Court case law. Anyone comparing the two would be quite surprised by the difference. But as the saying goes, "The Constitution is what the Supreme Court says it is." Surprisingly, the same is true for the Bible. It is what the interpreters say it is, whether the early church fathers, the reformers, or the popes. If you don't think so, see whether you can find Christmas, complete with gift-giving and Santa Claus, in the Scriptures. Find a command to wage war in the New Testament. Look for the encouragement to gain worldly wealth and power. Find the educated clergy and silent laity. None are there, but rather, just the opposite.   [20] As Roger Williams put it, "The Christian Church or Kingdom of the Saints, that Stone cut out of the mountain without human hands, (Daniel 2) now made all one with the mountain or Civil State, the Roman Empire, from whence it is cut or taken: Christ's lilies, garden and love, all one with the thorns, daughters and wilderness of the World." [*Bloudy Tenent of Persecution for Cause of Conscience* (1644), p. 174]   [21] *Transformation* — a complete change, usually into something with an improved appearance or usefulness; a permanent change in the genetic makeup of a cell when it acquires foreign DNA.   [22] Eusebius, *The Church History of Eusebius*, Book X, Chapters VI, which Frank Slaughter expounds on: "At the time of the Edict of Milan, the *clerici*, or clergy, had been recognized as a separate class of individuals and freed from many of the onerous duties devolving upon Roman citizens. As a result, there had been an immediate rush of wealthy people into the ranks of the clergy and from time to time it had been necessary to issue edicts controlling this trend." (Slaughter, *Constantine — The Miracle of the Flaming Cross*)   [23] This is where the word *liturgy* came from! "The service of the state (*leitourgia*) became the ritual, or liturgy, of the church;" and "the decree of the assembly and the opinions of the philosophers (*dogma*) became the fixed opinion of Christianity;" and "the correct opinion (*orthe doxa*) about things became orthodoxy." [*Encyclopedia Brittanica*, Macropaedia, Vol 12, p. 785 (1979)]

believed that a united and loyal church would ensure God's blessings on the entire empire.

A New God, a New Sign

One of the main reasons the religion of Christianity became the favored religion of governors and emperors was that it allowed Christians to be totally involved in nearly everything that any average citizen of the empire was involved in. Constantine groomed Christianity as his "pet religion" because of its docile, compromising nature. While in the past the church had been persecuted for its stance against the Empire's evils, it was now accepted as both church and empire "turned over a new leaf" in their development.

It was no little change when the "pinch of incense" previous emperors had demanded (but usually not received) was now freely given for the sake of imperial protection and support. Indeed, what other emperors had never gained from Christians by the sword — the recognition of their own divinity — the church now freely gave to Constantine! As the Catholic Encyclopedia article on Constantine the Great puts it:

> The imperial power was increased by receiving a religious consecration. The Church tolerated the cult of the emperor under many forms. It was permitted to speak of the divinity of the emperor, of the sacred palace, the sacred chamber and of the altar of the emperor, without being considered on this account an idolater... For what his predecessors had aimed to attain by the use of all their authority and at the cost of incessant bloodshed, was in truth only the recognition of their own divinity; Constantine gained this end, though he renounced the offering of sacrifices to himself. Some bishops, blinded by the splendor of the court, even went so far as to laud the emperor as an angel of God, as a sacred being, and to prophesy that he would, like the Son of God, reign in heaven.[24]

Thus, as the American visionary Roger Williams wrote, "Christianity fell asleep in the bosom of Constantine, and the laps and bosoms of those Emperors who professed the name of Christ."[25]

In this sleepy state, the distinction between Christians and non-Christians was broken down, and more and more pagans became "believers," since Christianity was now the favored religion, offering a greater hope of worldly success and prosperity. Nor was Constantine insensitive to the vast pagan population of his empire. To ease their way into his new, but up-and-coming Roman religion, Constantine set aside the "venerable day of the Sun" as the official day of rest of the Roman

[24] Herbermann, C., & Grupp, G. (1908). "Constantine the Great" in the *Catholic Encyclopedia*. NY: Robert Appleton Company. Retrieved June 23, 2010 from *http://www.newadvent.org/cathen/04295c.htm*   [25] Williams, *Bloudy Tenent*, p. 184

Empire. This was the first day of the week, which we know as Sunday, and the day on which most of his people already worshiped the sun god.[26] He did this in A.D. 321 in the following very clear words:

> On the venerable day of the Sun let the magistrates and people residing in cities rest, and let all workshops be closed.[27]

> In taking away the sign of the Sabbath, ironically, Constantine was an instrument of God to do His will.

But it was no mere political concern that empowered Constantine... something far greater was at work. In *this* act, ironically, Constantine was an *instrument of God* to do His will. In taking the sign of the Sabbath down he was only proclaiming what had long been true — that Christians were no longer God's people, loving His word and keeping His commandments — including the Ten Commandments! The fourth commandment, the longest of the ten, is certainly more than a mere "jot or tittle" of the Law, the setting aside of which makes you least in the kingdom of heaven.[28] The Ten Commandments were, according to Exodus 34:28, "the very words of the covenant" between God and His people. And the Sabbath was explicitly "a sign between Me and you throughout your generations, that you may know that I am the Lord who sanctifies you."[29]

Therefore, changing the day of rest could only be done by the authority of "another Jesus" and "another spirit," as Paul warned in 2 Corinthians 11:4. The authority of the gentle Lamb of God, who came "not to destroy men's lives but to save them,"[30] was set aside for the *new savior* — the one who proclaimed from the heavens on the eve of battle, "In *this* sign, conquer." Truly, Constantine "did not know what manner of spirit"[31] he was of to think that the Savior was validating or commanding the killing of those He came to save. Tragically, those who should have known better enthusiastically joined Constantine in his quest for world dominion. Those who gain the whole world lose their own soul.[32]

---

[26] "Sun worship with its Sun-day became dominant in Rome and in other parts of the Empire from the early part of the second century A.D. The Invincible Sun-god became the chief god of the Roman Pantheon and was worshiped especially on the Dies Solis, that is, "the Day of the Sun," known in our calendar as Sunday." Essay by S. Bacchiocchi, "From Sabbath to Sunday: How Did It Come About?" [27] *Codex Justinianus* lib. 3, tit. 12, 3; trans. in Philip Schaff, *History of the Christian Church*, Vol. 3, p. 380, note 1. [28] Matthew 5:17-19 [29] Exodus 31:13 [30] Luke 9:56 [31] Luke 9:55, which was said when His own apostles wanted to call fire down on the Samaritans for their insulting treatment of the Savior. [32] Luke 9:23-26

Proclaiming the day of the Sun to be the new day of rest for Rome, Constantine and the church leadership were busy creating a new religion, one the world calls Christianity. And this new sign of who God's people are has taken hold the world over, hasn't it? Constantine's "venerable day of the Sun" is everywhere recognized as the set-apart day of Christians — no less than the Jewish Sabbath, or Friday as the Muslim day of prayer.[33] As one encyclopedia article notes:

> Thus, Constantine, who had been a pagan solar worshiper, now looked upon the Christian deity as a bringer of victory. Persecution of the Christians was ended, and Constantine's co-emperor, Licinius, joined him in issuing the Edict of Milan (313), which mandated toleration of Christians in the Roman Empire. As guardian of Constantine's favored religion, the church was then given legal rights and large financial donations.[34]

Hailed as the deliverer and emancipator of the church, Constantine was then and still is viewed as a savior, securing the church's position in the world that would span the centuries. Most of the Christianized world today is content with the doctrines of faith that came down through the spiritual lineage of a nationally recognized Roman religion, never questioning very deeply the roots of their Christian religion or the foundation of the gospel they have trusted in. The legacy of Constantine is a church at one with the world that it was commissioned to call others out of. That legacy remains.

So, is this intimate cooperation and compromise with worldly power a good tree from which to pick good fruit? The Son of God said that a tree is known by the fruit it produces.[35] He said His disciples would be known by their love.[36] And this love is what all the Law and the Prophets hang on, as the Savior said:

> You shall love the LORD your God with all your heart, with all your soul, and with all your mind. This is the first and great commandment. And the second is like it: You shall love your neighbor as yourself. On these two commandments hang all the Law and the Prophets. (Matthew 22:37-40)

Not only did He come to fulfill the Law and Prophets;[37] but obviously, He commands us to fulfill them also. Therefore His words condemn both Constantine and Christianity, and all who claim to believe in Him are exposed as false if they do not keep these words: loving God with all their heart, soul, and strength, and in the same way, loving their neighbor as themselves. ❉

---

[33] There are some "Sabbath-keeping" Christians around the world, but they are a tiny minority of her two billion strong. As they themselves would admit, they live lives virtually indistinguishable from their neighbors. [34] "Constantine the Great," *Encarta 2000.* [35] Matthew 7:16-20 [36] John 13:34-35 [37] Matthew 5:17-19

UPON THIS ROCK

Simon Peter answered and said,
"You are the Christ, the Son of the living God."
Jesus answered and said to him, "Blessed are you, Simon Bar-Jonah,
for flesh and blood has not revealed this to you, but My Father who is in
heaven. And I also say to you that you are Peter, and on this rock I will build
My church, and the gates of Hades shall not prevail against it."
(Matthew 16:16-18)

Many have quoted this verse to prove the impossibility of the gates of Hades (the realm of the dead) prevailing against the church. They assume that regardless of the spiritual and moral condition of the church, God has never withdrawn His Holy Spirit from her, for a body without a spirit is dead, and that would mean the gates of death had prevailed against the church. But this is not what Yahshua was promising to Peter that day.

What Yahshua confirmed in Peter was that he was hearing from the Father — receiving revelation — not merely repeating what other men might have said. Peter had heard in his heart that Yahshua was the Messiah, and that revelation caused him to pledge his utter devotion and obedience to Him. Now that was something Yahshua could work with — people who could hear from His Father and obey what they heard. Upon such revelation He could build an eternal dwelling place for His Father's Spirit, for that, after all, is what the church is supposed to be (Eph 2:20-22).

The Master said things like this to His disciples many times, such as in this familiar passage:

> *Everyone then who hears these words of mine and does them will be like a wise man who built his house on the rock. And the rain fell, and the floods came, and the winds blew and beat on that house, but it did not fall, because it had been founded on the rock. And everyone who hears these words of mine and does not do them will be like a foolish man who built his house on the sand. And the rain fell, and the floods came, and the winds blew and beat against that house, and it fell, and great was the fall of it.*
> *(Matthew 7:24-27)*

Hearing and obeying is the foundation of the house that will endure all that comes against it, and wise is the man who builds on that rock. But foolish is the man who builds his house on those who hear but *do not obey*. That house will not withstand the test. The floods of deception and the shifting winds of doctrine will prevail against that house.

So was Yahshua, the Son of the Living God, a wise man or a foolish man? Was He contradicting Himself by saying that the house He was building would endure *regardless* of whether it was built on the foundation of hearing and obeying His words?

Many years later, in the waning days of the first-century church, the writer of Hebrews said these words to the church:

> But Christ was faithful as a Son over His house — whose house we are, **if** we hold fast our confidence and the boast of our hope firm until the end. (Hebrews 3:6)

The Greek word translated as "confidence" literally means *freedom in speaking; unreservedness in speech*. It is an outspokenness that comes from the confidence that one is hearing and obeying Messiah's words. Such outspokenness characterized the gatherings of the early church (1 Cor 14:26), when they were devoted to the apostles' teachings, but as the first century drew to a close and the churches were drifting from the simplicity of their first devotion (2 Cor 11:3-4), their gatherings degenerated to rote ritual and a professional clergy. That is the record of history. So, were they still "His house" in spite of Hebrews 3:6?

Here is another promise the Master made to His disciples:

> He who has My commandments and keeps them is the one who loves Me; and he who loves Me will be loved by My Father, and I will love him and will reveal Myself to him… If anyone loves me, he will keep My word, and My Father will love him, and we will come to him and make our home with him. (John 14:21,23)

Those who truly love Him obey Him, and He reveals Himself to them, which causes them to love and obey Him all the more. It is with such as these that He makes His home. He went on to say, "Whoever does not love Me does not keep My words." What can be said about them? Are they also His dwelling place? ❁

> If anyone does not love the Lord, let him be accursed. (1 Corinthians 16:22)

THE
INCUMBENCY

"And this good news of the kingdom will be proclaimed throughout the world as a testimony to all the nations, and then the end will come." (Matthew 24:14)

What *is* the good news of the kingdom, and how can it be proclaimed as a testimony to all the nations?

- A *testimony* or witness is the presentation of evidence or proof of something from one's first-hand experience.

- A *kingdom* is the domain of a king — where his commands are obeyed and his subjects enjoy his provision and protection.

- The *good news* is that the good King of this kingdom rescued us from slavery to the evil king of this present darkness.

He put His love (i.e., His Spirit) in our hearts so that we could love one another the same way He loved us. So to proclaim this good news as a witness or testimony to the nations means not just to speak, but for those who proclaim it to live together in every place just as they did in Jerusalem in Acts 2 and 4. This witness is for the King's subjects to make their first-hand experience of His love visible to the surrounding world by living together in love and unity:

"A new commandment I give to you, that you love one another; as I have loved you, that you also love one another. By this all will know that you are My disciples, if you have love for one another." (John 13:34-35)

"The glory which You have given Me I have given to them, that they may be one, just as We are one; I in them and You in Me, that they may be perfected in unity, so that the world may know that You sent Me, and loved them, even as You have loved Me." (John 17:22-23)

If this were ever to be done throughout the world over a period of several generations with increasing rather than decreasing zeal and consistency, it would bring about the end of the age, the *Jubilee*,[1] even the "acceptable year" Isaiah the prophet spoke of. Then Yahshua could return to judge righteously all those who despised the demonstration of His rule and persecuted His people. But this demonstration can only come about by His people being devoted to it, as Paul urged:

I therefore, a prisoner for the Lord, urge you to walk in a manner worthy of the calling to which you have been called, with all humility and gentleness, with patience, bearing with one another in love, eager to maintain the unity of the Spirit in the bond of peace. (Ephesians 4:1-3)

Except for a short time in the first century when the church was as described in Acts 2:44-47 and 4:32-35, this has never been done. Love left and doctrine took over. But since love *is* the Spirit,[2] which fulfills the Law,[3] so shall love also produce the right doctrine. However, doctrine does not, cannot, never has, and never will produce love.

It all began with Romans 5:5,

Now hope does not disappoint, because the love of God has been poured out in our hearts by the Holy Spirit who was given to us.

and 1 John 2:15 and 3:17 is how it all stopped:

Do not love the world or the things in the world. If anyone loves the world, the love of the Father is not in him. … Whoever has this world's goods, and sees his brother in need, and shuts up his heart from him, how does the love of God abide in him?

Since the first century, the world has not seen the love of 1 John 3:16 and John 13:34-35, which makes the unity of John 17:23 happen — being one as the Father and the Son are one. In order for the church to be restored, Acts 2 and 4 must be restored, and this takes a community, and a community takes love. God Himself is this kind of love, without which community is a useless endeavor done only in man's own strength and

---

[1] Isaiah 61:1-2, as the ultimate prophetic fulfillment of Leviticus 25:8-10
[2] 1 John 4:8   [3] Romans 8:4

46

ingenuity, i.e., *the flesh*. For true community to happen, the flesh must be crucified, which is what Yahshua was talking about when He said,

> *"Whoever desires to come after Me, let him deny himself, and take up his cross, and follow Me. For whoever desires to save his life will lose it, but whoever loses his life for My sake and the gospel's will save it." (Mark 8:34-35)*

This is the secret no one knows except those who know they have passed out of eternal death and into eternal life:

> *"Truly, truly, I say to you, whoever hears My word and believes Him who sent Me has eternal life. He does not come into judgment, but has passed from death into life." (John 5:24)*

Many Christians quote this verse, but they don't quote the *litmus test*[4] that goes with it:

> *We know that we have passed out of death and into life because we love the brothers. Whoever does not love abides in death... By this we know love: that He laid down His life for us, and we ought to lay down our lives for the brothers. (1 John 3:14,16)*

> *If anyone says, "I love God," and hates [i.e., does not love] his brother, he is a liar; for he who does not love his brother whom he has seen cannot love God whom he has not seen. (1 John 4:20)*

When disciples are laying down their lives for one another in love, they have confidence from the Holy Spirit[5] that they have passed out of death and into life. Therefore, they are outspoken in the gatherings, for that life bubbles out of them continually in thanksgiving and encouragement.[6] Obviously, the Apostle Paul expected the churches under his care to be known for the full participation of every disciple:

> *What then, brothers? When you come together, each one has a hymn, a lesson, a revelation, another language, or an interpretation. Let all things be done for building up. (1 Corinthians 14:26)*

There were no professional preachers, musicians, or choir directors. As Paul told the Ephesians, he also expected this full participation, motivated by love, to characterize their whole lives, whether in the gatherings or not:

> *Speaking the truth in love, we are to grow up in every aspect [of our personality[7]] into Him who is the head, into Christ, from whom the whole*

---

[4] See *The Litmus Test* on page 127. [5] 1 John 3:24 [6] John 7:37-39; 1 Peter 4:11
[7] The five aspects of our personality: physical, spiritual, mental, emotional, and social.

body, *joined and held together by every joint with which it is equipped, when each part is working properly, makes the body grow so that it builds itself up in love. (Ephesians 4:15-16)*

Paul's last exhortation to the church in Ephesus was, "Grace be with all those who love our Lord Jesus Christ with incorruptible, undying love."[8] Yet less than 40 years later, Yahshua Himself had this to say to that same church: "I have this against you, that you have abandoned the love you had at first."[9] It didn't take long before the corruption set in hard and fast, expressing the incumbency of the Nicolaitan system — the system that God hates.[10]

The Incumbency: Church Politics

Incumbency is the period during which an office is held. It is a well-known fact of the political process that it is hard to unseat an incumbent office-holder. Once someone attains to a position of power or influence, it can be very difficult to remove him from office. He uses his power and influence to make the people dependent on him. As it is in politics, so it became in the church.

The word *Nicolaitan* is derived from *nikao*, meaning "to conquer," and *laos*, meaning "people," hence, "people conquerors." In the waning years of the first century church, as their love grew cold, most grew silent while leaders rose up and filled the vacuum with their persuasive and eloquent monologues.[11] It was just as Paul had warned the Ephesian elders:

I know that after my departure fierce wolves will come in among you, not sparing the flock; and from among your own selves will arise men speaking twisted things, to draw away the disciples after themselves. (Acts 20:29-30)

Already, by the end of the first century, the Nicolaitan system had appeared in Ephesus[12] and had made significant headway in Pergamum.[13] It was an evil system of Satan that infiltrated the church.[14] When the last of the overcomers[15] died, there was no longer a way for the Holy Spirit to express Himself.[16] Messiah was no longer the head over *that* house,[17] where the common people had lost their love and outspokenness:

But Christ as a Son over His own house, whose house we are if we hold fast the confidence and the rejoicing of the hope firm to the end. (Hebrews 3:6)

---

[8] Ephesians 6:24   [9] Revelation 2:4   [10] Revelation 2:6,15   [11] 2 Corinthians 11:3-6
[12] Revelation 2:6   [13] Revelation 2:15   [14] 1 John 4:1-5; John 12:26; 14:18,20
[15] Revelation 3:4-5   [16] 1 Corinthians 3:16   [17] James 1:26-27; 2:19; Revelation 2:5; Romans 11:22

The fullest expression of the Nicolaitan System

The Greek word for confidence means outspokenness, freedom – even unreservedness of speech. When that outspokenness ceased among the people, according to the Word of God, Christ ceased being the High Priest over that silent house. The result of the conquest of the Nicolaitans is the clergy-laity system, which is a misnomer. "Conquerors of the People" is a more fitting name for this evil religious system.

Nicolaitanism was a doctrine that crept into their midst like an unclean thing from the dark lagoon. It came from the incumbency of those who saw leadership not as the Master had taught (shepherds who daily laid down their life for the sheep[18]), but as a position to hold. To incubate their self-perpetuating eggs the Nicolaitans led the pew-sitters to sit contentedly (silently) on them until they hatched — a brood of serpents, just as the leaders of the Jews had been called by John the Baptist.[19] To hatch these Nicolaitan eggs took the artificial heat needed to maintain the ideal temperature for the optimal growth and development of bacterial cultures — *lukewarm*.[20]

Incubation is the period of time between the exposure to an infectious disease and the appearance of the symptoms. To sit on eggs is to foster incubation. An incubator is an apparatus kept at uniform warmth. The lukewarm church itself became an incubator for the artificial hatching of the Nicolaitan eggs that Satan laid right before their undiscerning spirits.

This Nicolaitan system was finally inculcated into the church by pressing it on their minds through repetition by frequent lectures and

[18] Luke 22:25-27   [19] Matthew 3:7   [20] Revelation 3:16

admonitions.[21] The churches became accustomed to listening to only one person instead of benefiting from the full participation of each member.[22] Under this persuasion, church members became their own prison guards, looking with suspicion on anyone outside the clergy who dared to speak up and express his heart. That's how effective the endless repetitions of the clergy were in thoroughly instilling the new doctrine into their minds.

So the one incumbent Nicolaitan in each church, who had arisen by smooth talk and manipulation,[23] tenaciously held onto his office and performed his official duties as an autocrat.[24] Diotrephes, whom John the Apostle wrote of in his third letter, set the pattern for centuries to come, putting out of the church any who were a threat to his position:

> I wrote to the church, but Diotrephes, who loves to have the preeminence among them, does not receive us. Therefore, if I come, I will call to mind his deeds which he does, prating against us with malicious words. And not content with that, he himself does not receive the brethren, and forbids those who wish to, putting them out of the church. (3 John 1:9-10)

Such incumbents encumber the sincere, hindering any action or motion toward godliness. They impose unreasonable burdens, the same heavy weights of outward righteousness for which Yahshua condemned the Pharisees. They bolster their own ego,[25] fed by Satan's pride, the very Nicolaitan spirit of self-exaltation that God hates.[26]

The Kingdom was shut out by the encumbering incumbents,[27] and only a few overcomers were left,[28] and they were probably put out of the church. The teachings of the Nicolaitans became an incurable deadly disease that killed the first church, spreading like gangrene or cancer, incurable, with no hope of reformation.[29] The unending incumbency of these men, filled with the devouring spirit of the evil one himself, snuffed out the light of the world. Then came Constantine to merge the church with the state when the fallen church was ripe for the picking.

The people were silenced due to the overwhelming insurgency[30] of the incumbent Nicolaitans, Satan's servants.[31] This ecclesiastical system was received by a passive laity due to the persuasion of the incumbent "office holders" – the clergy in their black robes. All authority in the church fell to them by default through the failure of the many to accept

---

[21] 2 Corinthians 11:4,15 [22] 1 Corinthians 14:26; Hebrews 3:6; 1 Peter 4:11; 1 Corinthians 11:5 [23] Acts 20:30 [24] Autocrat — a ruler who has absolute power; a domineering person. [25] Matthew 23:4 [26] Revelation 2:6,15 [27] Matthew 23:13 [28] Revelation 3:4 [29] It is futile to try to reform something that is dead, which is all the Reformation of the 16th century did. There was no restoration of the life of the first-century church, but merely a reformation of the apostate religion of dead ritual. *Apostate* means departed from the apostles' teaching to which the first disciples were devoted (Acts 2:42). [30] Insurgent — *adj.*, rising in active revolt; *n.*, a rebel or revolutionary [31] 3 John 1:9; 2 Corinthians 11:3,4,13-15

the responsibility of their priesthood. Due to the general lack of wisdom, understanding, discernment, insight, discretion, and faithfulness to pray to be delivered from evil,[32] the church was taken captive. None who joined from that time on received the Holy Spirit, but all the while they claimed to see.[33]

They could memorize John 5:24 quite well, and were mesmerized by John 3:16, but were strangely unconcerned with 1 John 3:16. Therefore, the kind of believing that resulted in Acts 2:44 was out of the question. (Yet Acts 2:44 remains the standard for *all* generations for *all* who *believe* with the kind of belief that John 3:16 is speaking of.)

> *So by the second century, James was regarded by them as the insurgent one, since he had the audacity to write to the church, "You believe that God is one; you do well. Even the demons believe — and shudder! But do you want to know, O foolish man, that faith without works is dead?"[34]*

Nightfall descended upon the true way to life, and truly, as the Savior said, no man could do the works of God.[35] This dead faith and the fallen incumbency, which has held the reigns of power for almost 1900 years, have been inseparable. Very early, the church left behind their roots in the ancient Hebrew faith[36] and the Jerusalem pattern of full participation in a life together, sharing all things in common.[37] They even abandoned the original Hebrew name of the Messiah, *Yahshua*, meaning "Yahweh's Salvation."[38] Instead, they adopted the Greek name *Iesous Christos* and became known as *Christianity*, characterized by a professional clergy and a largely passive laity. Little or no participation or accountability was required of its members beyond their attendance and tithes, and their assent to a doctrinal creed.[39] The resulting rampant hypocrisy grieves the few who still long for the vibrant life of the first-century church.

But there is Good News! That life is sprouting again on the earth! Anyone who is willing to do God's will can become a full participant in the way of life of our good King, Yahshua, the Messiah. It is a life based not on doctrine but on love, following the ancient pattern of the early church. We invite you to overthrow the incumbency of dead religion in your own life and join the true commonwealth of Israel, God's holy nation.[40] Here everyone has a voice and a vocation to give their all in building up the witness of the coming Kingdom[41] as a foretaste of the age to come. This will actually bring about the end of this wicked age and the return of the Messiah to establish His Kingdom on earth.[42] ♣

---

[32] Matthew 6:13   [33] John 9:41; 1 John 2:4   [34] James 2:19-20; See also *The Insurgent* on page 21.   [35] John 9:5   [36] Romans 11:17-21   [37] Acts 2:42-47; 1 Thessalonians 2:14   [38] For more about this name, see *The Name above all Names* on page 151.   [39] See also *The Paradigm Shift from Community to Doctrine* on page 135.   [40] Ephesians 2:12; Galatians 6:16; 1 Peter 2:9-10   [41] 1 Peter 2:9-10   [42] Matthew 24:14

THE FOUNDATIONS
OF THE
GOSPEL OF THE KINGDOM

*The Gospel preached by Yahshua was not
His own invention, nor was it a radical departure
from what God had spoken since He called Abraham
out of Ur. On the contrary, everything that Yahshua
spoke came forth from His deep understanding
of the Scriptures, the nature of man,
and the heart of His Father.
Apart from this foundation
the Gospel cannot be fully understood.
In fact, it has been misunderstood and misrepresented
by Christianity for the past 1900 years.*

*The articles in this section reveal
the roots of the Gospel in the Old Testament
and its radical implications for those who aspire
to be Yahshua's disciples today.*

Where did the Gospel Come From?

What does the return of the Jews from Babylon, and Abraham's call to leave Ur and go to the Promised Land have to do with the Gospel? EVERYTHING!

For forty years, the "weeping prophet" Jeremiah had warned his people of the judgment that was coming upon them for their idolatry and rebellion, but few heeded his message. When the armies of King Nebuchadnezzar of Babylon finally surrounded and laid siege to the city in 586 BC, it was too late to repent. Jerusalem was laid waste, the Temple destroyed, and all but the poorest survivors were carried away to Babylon where Jeremiah had prophesied they would remain for 70 years.[1]

But Jeremiah had also given them the hope of returning to their land when their time of discipline was over, and it is thrilling to read of the Persian conquest of Babylon at the end of those 70 years, and their release from captivity by King Cyrus:

> In the first year of Cyrus king of Persia, that the word of the LORD by the mouth of Jeremiah might be fulfilled, the LORD stirred up the spirit of Cyrus king of Persia, so that he made a proclamation throughout all his kingdom and also put it in writing: "Thus says Cyrus king of Persia: The LORD, the God of heaven, has given me all the kingdoms of the earth, and He has charged me to build Him a house at Jerusalem, which is in Judah. Whoever is among you of all His people, may his God be with him, and let him go up to Jerusalem, which is in Judah, and rebuild the house of the LORD, the God of Israel — He is the God who is in Jerusalem. (Ezra 1:1-3)

What an amazing fulfillment of prophecy! You can go on to read of their return to rebuild the Temple, followed by the exciting story of how Nehemiah rallied the people to rebuild the city walls in only 52 days, despite intense opposition. It would be quite reasonable to envision all the

---

[1] The seventy years of Jeremiah's prophecy began with the "good figs" of Jeremiah 24 that Nebuchadnezzar carried away in his first conquest of Jerusalem. They were "the best and brightest Jews" the historian Ken Shapiro refers to below — King Jeconiah, his officials, and the craftsman and smiths of Jerusalem. The years would end in 536 BC with the edict of Cyrus recorded in Ezra 1.

exiles bursting forth from their long captivity to return to their beloved city and rebuild her walls and restore her former glory.

By the Waters of Babylon

But a closer look at history reveals the shocking fact that there were about one million Jews living in Babylon at the end of their 70-year exile, and fewer than 50,000 returned to Jerusalem. Less than 5 percent! Why did so few respond? The sad truth is that more than 95 percent preferred the comforts of their life in Babylon to the sufferings of returning and rebuilding Jerusalem[2] and restoring the life of God in the one place on earth He had chosen for His name to dwell.[3]

As one historian put it, after arriving in the land of their exile, "… they forged a new national identity and a new religion."[4]

> In the first foray, the Babylonians did not destroy the Temple, nor send the Jews into exile. However, they did succeed in taking into captivity 10,000 of the best and brightest Jews. While it seemed like a terrible disaster at the time, these brilliant men, Torah scholars all, immediately established a Jewish infrastructure upon arrival in Babylon. A dozen years later when the Temple was destroyed, the Jews who were exiled to Babylon found there yeshivas, synagogues, kosher butchers, etc., all the essentials for maintaining a Jewish life…[5]

… all except the Temple sacrifices, that is, which were their only means of being forgiven of their sins. Thus the synagogue was born to soothe the guilty consciences of a people banished from their land for their rebellion and idolatry, while their sins piled up as high as heaven. Once a week, they would gather to be led through a ritual of psalms, prayers, and readings from the Law which they had spurned and the Prophets which they had ignored. At first they mourned, as the psalmist wrote:

> By the waters of Babylon, there we sat down and wept,
>   when we remembered Zion.
> On the willows there we hung up our harps.
> For there our captors required of us songs,
>   and our tormentors, mirth, saying,
>   "Sing us one of the songs of Zion!"
> How shall we sing Yahweh's song in a foreign land?

[2] Rabbi Ken Spiro, "Crash Course in Jewish History #24 – Purim in Persia," http://www.aish.com/literacy/jewishhistory. See also Josephus, Antiquities of the Jews (11.8). [3] Deuteronomy 12:13-14; 16:2,5,6; Nehemiah 1:8-9; 1 Kings 11:36; 14:21
[4] http://www.jewishvirtuallibrary.org/jsource/History/Exile.html
[5] Ken Spiro, "Crash Course in Jewish History #43 – Jews in Babylon," http://www.aish.com/literacy/jewishhistory

If I forget you, O Jerusalem,
  let my right hand forget its skill!
Let my tongue stick to the roof of my mouth,
  if I do not remember you,
    if I do not set Jerusalem above my highest joy!
      (Psalm 137:1-6)

But somewhere along the way they stopped mourning, and moved on to making the most of their circumstances. Indeed, their fertile flocks, fruitful fields, and financial finesse carved out a comfortable niche for them in the land of their captivity. They built more schools and more synagogues that nurtured a new generation who were quite content with a mythical Jerusalem and a mystical religion far removed from the simple faith of their father Abraham who had left that very land so long ago.

The Faith of Abraham

Abraham had looked up at the very same stars that shone over their heads, longing to know the One who had filled the expanse of heaven with such glory, and longing to know the purpose for his existence. He was not content with the rich life of Ur, nestled in the fertile floodplain of the Tigris and Euphrates rivers, or even Haran where his family settled for a time. That is why his heart could be stirred by the Spirit of his Creator, and that is why he had ears to hear the voice that said, "Go from your country and your kindred and your father's house to the land that I will show you."[6]

---

[6] Genesis 12:1

How fond and tender must have been the farewells of Abraham as he kissed his loved ones goodbye forever, placed his life in the care of his God, and set his face toward an unknown land! Abraham did not shrink back from leaving all behind — family, friends, and material security — to follow that voice to the land of promise. His faith caused him to obey God.

1,500 years later, that same voice called out to Abraham's wayward offspring to leave that same land of worldly comfort and return to the same land of heavenly promise, but only a few responded — only those whose hearts could still be stirred.[7] And just like Abraham, they left everything behind to follow that voice — family, friends, possessions, plans, comfort, and security — in order to restore the desolate heritage of Abraham and redeem the name of his God.

To the rest — almost a million Jews — the good news of release from their captivity did not sound so good. In fact, it was the fragrance of death to them, not the fragrance of life.[8] Surely (or so they thought), their God was not so unreasonable as to expect them to *literally* leave everything they had worked so hard to establish, since He had so obviously blessed them, not only materially, but also with a rich social and religious life. It was fine for the adventurous few to risk their lives on a long and dangerous journey, and wear themselves out trying to restore what lay in ruins. But they could worship their God just as well in Babylon (or so they thought), and in their hearts they would take identity with their zealous brothers in Jerusalem, and send their tithes and offerings. After all, who

[7] Ezra 1:3,5   [8] 2 Corinthians 2:16

would finance the work if they were all so reckless as to leave everything for which they had labored?

The New Religion of the Jews

Meanwhile, the new religion of Judaism (not to be confused with the obedient faith of Abraham) continued to flourish in the land of Babylon, its spiritual center, independent of the restored Temple worship in Jerusalem. They even chose their own ruler from the line of King David, who, although he was not called a king, was recognized as their nobleman by the Persian government.[9] This new "Davidic dynasty" continued in Babylon for over 1,500 years.[10] By the end of that time, their rabbinic academy had compiled every jot and tittle of their new religion into what became known as the *Babylonian Talmud*, the most authoritative document of Judaism, eclipsing even the Torah itself. To them, only through the lens of their published commentaries could the Torah be properly understood and applied.

The Jewish religion that had incubated in Babylon was inevitably carried back to Jerusalem by the courageous few who returned, so that even after the Temple was rebuilt and the ministry of the Levitical priesthood restored, what emanated from it was at best a diluted mixture — a few parts Abraham's faith and many parts "essence of Babylon." Five hundred years later, at the dawn of the first century AD, all that

[9] Ken Spiro, "Crash Course in Jewish History #43 – Jews in Babylon," *http://www.aish.com/literacy/jewishhistory*   [10] Until about 1000 AD.

remained was lifeless ritual and a handful of faithful men and women suffering under the control of a religious elite who had carved out a comfortable niche for themselves under Roman rule.

Virtual Babylon

Under Roman rule, the Jews were effectively exiles in their own land, a virtual Babylon, where they were allowed to practice their religion as long as it was no threat to their Roman overlords. And it was no threat as long as there were no prophets stirring up the people and reminding them of who they were supposed to be and what they were supposed to do as God's holy people. The last true prophet of Israel had been Malachi, over 400 years earlier, who had denounced their corrupt priesthood and the lame sacrifices being offered up in the Temple only a few decades after its restoration, expressing the cry of God's heart:

> *"Oh, that there were one among you who would shut the doors, that you might not kindle fire on My altar in vain! I have no pleasure in you," says the LORD of hosts, "and I will not accept an offering from your hand. For from the rising of the sun to its setting My name will be great among the nations, and in every place incense will be offered to My name, and a pure offering. For My name will be great among the nations," says the LORD of hosts. (Malachi 1:10-11)*

It was a shocking thing to say, seemingly contradicting the clear instruction given in the Law that the priestly sacrifices could only be offered up in the one place their God had caused His name to dwell, namely in Jerusalem.[11] It was a "wake up" call to what was left of the holy nation, letting them know that if they didn't repent He would look elsewhere for a holy people — beyond the borders of Israel.[12] He would do exactly what Moses himself had prophesied:

> *They have made me jealous with what is no god; they have provoked me to anger with their idols. So I will make them jealous with those who are no people; I will provoke them to anger with a foolish nation. (Deut 32:21)[13]*

Malachi went on to speak of a messenger who would come in the spirit of Elijah to prepare the way for the Messiah. That messenger was John the Baptist, who had these opening words for the descendants of the corrupt priests of Malachi's day:

> *"You brood of vipers! Who warned you to flee from the wrath to come? Bear fruit in keeping with repentance. And do not presume to say to yourselves, 'We have Abraham as our father,' for I tell you, God is able from these stones to raise up children for Abraham. Even now the ax is*

---

[11] Deuteronomy 12:13-14; 16:2,5,6; 1 Kings 11:36; 14:21   [12] Malachi 1:5
[13] Romans 10:19; 11:11-14; 1 Peter 2:9-10

laid to the root of the trees. Every tree therefore that does not bear good fruit is cut down and thrown into the fire." (Matthew 3:7-10)

John merely spoke the plain truth: Even though they were physically in the land and offering sacrifices in the Temple, spiritually they were just as far removed from the life and heart of God as if they were still in Babylon. Their lame sacrifices were not accepted and their sins were piling up to heaven. The sharp rebuke sent shivers through the sensitive few who hated the religious hypocrisy and economic injustice all around them. Their hearts were stirred by this prophet, and they longed for the Messiah whom John said would soon appear to bring the remedy.

The Remedy

It is impossible to understand the purpose of Messiah's coming, the meaning of His message, and the significance of His death and resurrection apart from the condition of Israel at that time, how it came to be that way, and how it was supposed to be. He did not come to provide a free ticket to heaven, but to redeem a people for His own possession who would do His Father's will on the earth. And that will had not changed.[14] His will was still the same as it had been for Abraham coming out of Ur, and for the twelve tribes coming out of Egypt, and for the Jews coming out of Babylon: that He would have a dwelling place in a holy people who would be a light to the nations[15] around them, showing them what He is really like by their love for one another.

As the prophet Isaiah put it, God wanted His people to be like a vineyard bearing the fruit of justice and righteousness.[16] In fact, in the last few days before the crucifixion, after driving the money-changers out of the Temple courts, Yahshua[17] retold Isaiah's parable of the vineyard to the chief priests and elders,[18] recounting Israel's repeated rebellion and extending it to how they would soon treat Him. Then He ended the story with the ringing judgment:

"Therefore I say to you, the kingdom of God will be taken from you and given to a nation bearing the fruits of it." (Matthew 21:43)

He went on to deliver a scathing condemnation of the fallen religious system in seven woes against the scribes and Pharisees, and to prophesy the utter destruction of the Temple.[19] At that point, they began to make plans to arrest Him. In demanding His crucifixion, they called a curse upon themselves and their children,[20] which has faithfully followed them down through the subsequent centuries.

---

[14] Malachi 3:6 [15] Isaiah 42:6; 49:6; 58:8,10; 60:3; Matthew 5:14-16; Acts 13:47 ("you" is plural in all these verses; it is the *corporate* light of a holy people)
[16] Isaiah 5:1-7; 27:6 [17] *Yahshua* is the Hebrew name of the Messiah; see *The Name Above all Names* on page 151. [18] Matthew 21:33-40 [19] Matthew 23:1-39; 24:2
[20] Matthew 27:25

But who was the nation to whom the Kingdom of God would be given, which was expected to bear the fruit of it? Did these words of the Messiah have anything to do with the gospel or "good news" of the Kingdom that He had been preaching since His baptism,[21] and which He said His disciples would also be preaching?

> "This Gospel of the Kingdom will be preached in all the world as a witness to all the nations, and then the end will come." (Matthew 24:14)

Could it have anything to do with the prophecy of Isaiah 49:6?

> "It is too small a thing that You should be My Servant to raise up the tribes of Jacob and to bring back the preserved of Israel; I will make You as a light for the nations, that My salvation may reach to the end of the earth." (Isaiah 49:6)

Since He told His disciples that everythingwritten about Him in the Law, the Prophets, and the Psalms must be fulfilled,[22] where and when was this prophecy fulfilled? Later, the apostle Paul quoted this very passage in support of his ministry,[23] and he also spoke of it in his defense before King Agrippa:

> "And now I stand here on trial because of my hope in the promise made by God to our fathers, to which our twelve tribes hope to attain, as they earnestly worship night and day. And for this hope I am accused by Jews, O king!" (Acts 26:6-7)

Paul was in trouble with the Jews because the gospel he preached was raising up a twelve-tribed spiritual Israel[24] from among the Gentiles,[25] beyond the borders of the land of Israel.[26] It was exactly what Yahshua, the Messiah, had said would happen — the Kingdom would be taken away from the Jews and given to a nation that would bear its fruit.[27] And it would happen as a result of the preaching of the Gospel of the Kingdom.

The Gospel of the Kingdom

> "This doctrine of the Kingdom of Heaven, which was the main teaching of Jesus, and which plays so small a part in the Christian creeds, is certainly one of the most revolutionary doctrines that ever stirred and changed human thought." ~ H. G. Wells[28]

[21] Matthew 4:23; 9:35; Mark 1:14-15 [22] Matthew 5:17-18; Luke 24:44-45
[23] Acts 13:47 [24] Isaiah 49:6; Ephesians 2:12; Galatians 3:29; 6:16 [25] Acts 13:46
— Paul's fervent hope was to move his fellow Jews to jealousy (Romans 10:19; 11:13-15; Deuteronomy 32:21), so that they would someday repent (Zechariah 12:10) and God could righteously fulfill His promise to give them the land, enemy-free, in the next age (Genesis 15:18-21; Luke 1:72-75). [26] Malachi 1:5,11
[27] Matthew 21:43 [28] H. G. Wells, *The Outline of History*, vol. 1, p. 422 (1961)

You may never have thought of the gospel as having anything to do with raising up a twelve-tribed nation in the midst of the nations of the earth to be a light to them. And you may never have considered that the gospel had anything to do with the Jews having been called out of Babylon to re-establish the physical nation of Israel. But the gospel that Yahshua and His apostles preached had *everything* to do with *both*.

Yahshua came to call His people out of Babylon to rebuild the Temple and restore the walls of Jerusalem. Of course, it was not the historical Babylon or the physical temple and city walls, but rather the spiritual realities that they represented. However, *spiritual* does not mean *mystical* or *invisible*. The building materials were *spiritual* men and women, and the building was both visible and tangible, as in the following verses:

> So the Jews said to Him, "What sign do you show us for doing these things?" Jesus answered them, "Destroy this temple, and in three days I will raise it up." The Jews then said, "It has taken forty-six years to build this temple, and will you raise it up in three days?" But He was speaking about the temple of His Body. When therefore He was raised from the dead, His disciples remembered that He had said this, and they believed the Scripture and the word that Jesus had spoken. (John 2:18-22)

> As you come to him, a living stone rejected by men but in the sight of God chosen and precious, you yourselves like living stones are being built up as a spiritual house, to be a holy priesthood, to offer spiritual sacrifices acceptable to God through Jesus Christ. (1 Peter 2:4-5)

> So then you are no longer strangers and aliens, but you are fellow citizens with the saints and members of the household of God, built on the foundation of the apostles and prophets, Christ Jesus himself being the cornerstone, in whom the whole structure, being joined together, grows into a holy temple in the Lord. In him you also are being built together into a dwelling place for God by the Spirit. (Ephesians 2:19-22)

> "Come, I will show you the Bride, the wife of the Lamb." And he carried me away in the Spirit to a great, high mountain, and showed me the holy city Jerusalem coming down out of heaven from God, having the glory of God, its radiance like a most rare jewel, like a jasper, clear as crystal. It had a great, high wall, with twelve gates, and at the gates twelve angels, and on the gates the names of the twelve tribes of the sons of Israel... And the wall of the city had twelve foundations, and on them were the twelve names of the twelve apostles of the Lamb. (Revelation 21:9-14)

But where did the building materials come from, and how were they gathered? The foundation stones came from the "Babylon" that Israel had become, and they were gathered in the same way that the Jews had been gathered out of Babylon of old: those whose hearts were stirred by the *good news* that it was time to restore the dwelling place of God on the

earth forsook everything to follow the One who was leading the way. They left family, friends, careers, and possessions to follow Yahshua, responding immediately to His call:

> While walking by the Sea of Galilee, he saw two brothers, Simon (who is called Peter) and Andrew his brother, casting a net into the sea, for they were fishermen. And he said to them, "Follow me, and I will make you fishers of men." Immediately they left their nets and followed him. And going on from there he saw two other brothers, James the son of Zebedee and John his brother, in the boat with Zebedee their father, mending their nets, and he called them. Immediately they left the boat and their father and followed him. (Matthew 4:18-22)

That same response was required of all who would follow Him, a fact which even took His first disciples by surprise when they heard His command to a wealthy, religious young man who was seeking eternal life:

> And Jesus, looking at him, loved him, and said to him, "You lack one thing: go, sell all that you have and give to the poor, and you will have treasure in heaven; and come, follow me." Disheartened by the saying, he went away sorrowful, for he had great possessions. And Jesus looked around and said to his disciples, "How difficult it will be for those who have wealth to enter the kingdom of God!"

> And the disciples were amazed at his words. But Jesus said to them again, "Children, how difficult it is to enter the kingdom of God! It is easier for a camel to go through the eye of a needle than for a rich person to enter the kingdom of God…"

And they were exceedingly astonished, and said to him, "Who then can be saved?" Peter began to say to him, "See, we have left everything and followed you."

Jesus said, "Truly, I say to you, there is no one who has left house or brothers or sisters or mother or father or wife or children or lands, for my sake and for the gospel, who will not receive a hundredfold now in this time, houses and brothers and sisters and mothers and children and lands, with persecutions, and in the age to come eternal life." (Mark 10:21-30)

Just as surely as it was impossible for anyone to obey the call to rebuild the Temple while remaining in Babylon (or even to drag his possessions and his unwilling family members along with him on the arduous 700-mile journey to Jerusalem), so it was impossible to follow the Messiah without forsaking one's life in this world, with all of its material and emotional trappings. And just as back then, most were unwilling to give up their comfort and security. But the Master's words were unyielding to the excuses of the unwilling:

A scribe came up and said to him, "Teacher, I will follow you wherever you go." And Jesus said to him, "Foxes have holes, and birds of the air have nests, but the Son of Man has nowhere to lay his head." Another of the disciples said to him, "Lord, let me first go and bury my father." And Jesus said to him, "Follow me, and leave the dead to bury their own dead." (Matthew 8:19-22)

"If anyone comes to Me and does not hate his own father and mother and wife and children and brothers and sisters, yes, and even his own life, he cannot be My disciple... Whoever of you does not forsake all that he has cannot be My disciple." (Luke 14:26,33)

"And whoever does not take his cross and follow Me is not worthy of Me." (Matthew 10:38)

"Whoever loves his life loses it, and whoever hates his life in this world will keep it for eternal life. If anyone serves Me, he must follow Me; and where I am, there will My servant be also. If anyone serves Me, the Father will honor him." (John 12:25-26)

Rebuilding the Temple

It wasn't that Yahshua was being hard or unreasonable. It was all a matter of where He was going and what He was building: He was going to the cross and into death in order to redeem those whom He would build into an eternal dwelling place for the Holy One of Israel.[29] With all His heart He wanted His Father to get the faithful, holy nation He always desired, and He wanted the world He loved so much to be able to see the heart of His Father through the witness of that holy nation[30] — redeemed human beings living together in unity,[31] loving one another as He had loved His disciples[32] which was 24 hours a day, 7 days a week. But in order for that to happen, they would all have to abandon their independent lives in "Babylon" and throw in their lot together in "Jerusalem."

That is exactly what happened on the day of Pentecost, ten days after Yahshua's ascension. Pierced to the heart by the words Peter spoke, 3000 people responded to his call to "be saved from this perverse generation"[33] by forsaking their old lives and banding together to form the nucleus of the new spiritual Israel:

> *Now all who believed were together, and had all things in common, and sold their possessions and goods, and divided them among all, as anyone had need. So continuing daily with one accord in the temple courts, and breaking bread from house to house, they ate their food with gladness and simplicity of heart... The multitude of those who believed were of one heart and one soul; neither did anyone say that any of the things he possessed was his own, but they had all things in common. And with great power the apostles gave witness to the resurrection of the Lord Jesus. And great grace was upon them all. Nor was there anyone among them who lacked; for all who were possessors of lands or houses sold them, and brought the proceeds of the things that were sold, and laid them at the apostles' feet; and they distributed to each as anyone had need. (Acts 2:44-46; 4:32-35)*

Now, many Christians say that this common life did not last, or even that it was a mistake that God Himself had to break up by sending persecution.[34] The second claim is ironically absurd, considering the response the Master gave to Peter when he said, "See, we have left everything and followed you."

---

[29] John 14:23; 2 Corinthians 6:16; Ephesians 2:22; Revelation 21:2-3
[30] Matthew 24:14 [31] John 17:21-23 [32] John 13:34-35 [33] Acts 2:37-40 [34] Acts 8:1

Jesus said, "Truly, I say to you, there is no one who has left house or brothers or sisters or mother or father or wife or children or lands, for my sake and for the gospel, who will not receive a hundredfold now in this time, houses and brothers and sisters and mothers and children and lands, **along with persecutions,** *and in the age to come eternal life." (Mark 10:29-30)*

What happened on the day of Pentecost was the very hundredfold blessing the Master had promised His disciples who had given up everything, and the persecution that resulted was part of His promise, not a punishment for their obedience. In fact, the Master had consistently taught them to expect persecution if they were faithful to Him.[35]

> ❧
>
> *What happened on the day of Pentecost was the very hundredfold blessing the Master had promised His disciples who had given up everything.*
>
> ❧

Furthermore, the hundredfold increase resulting from the wholehearted surrender of disciples was the very means by which the holy nation[36] would be built as they gave up their homes and farms, which were either sold to meet the pressing needs of existing communities[37] or became the open door to starting new communities. In the same way that a beehive, when it fills up, sends out a swarm to start a new hive,[38] so the early church multiplied, replicating the pattern of the first community in Jerusalem, and experiencing the same persecution as a result of it.[39]

As for the claim that the common life of the early church didn't last, that is sadly true, although it lasted much longer than most Christians think. What destroyed it was not persecution from without, but corruption from within. As long as all were full participants in their common life, with each member walking in the works prepared for him[40] and speaking the very utterances of God by the grace and strength He provided,[41] the spiritual temple continued to be built.[42] They were truly a spiritual priesthood[43] serving under a faithful High Priest,[44] and their spiritual sacrifices were acceptable to God.[45] But gradually, self-concern[46] crept in like a deadly cancer, cooling off their original fervent love for one another,[47] and taking away their confidence[48] and outspokenness[49] until they were no longer qualified to be called His house:

[35] John 15:18-21; 16:1-2; Luke 6:26 [36] 1 Peter 2:9; Ephesians 2:12 [37] Acts 4:37
[38] See *Like a Beehive* on page 179. [39] 1 Thessalonians 2:14 [40] Ephesians 2:10
[41] 1 Peter 4:10-11 [42] Ephesians 4:15-16; Colossians 2:19 [43] 1 Peter 2:9
[44] Hebrews 3:1-2 [45] Romans 12:1; Hebrews 13:15-16 [46] Philippians 2:3-4,
NRSV (other versions water it down) [47] 1 Peter 4:8; Revelation 2:4 [48] 1 John
3:14,16-22 [49] 1 Corinthians 14:24-26

But Christ was faithful as a Son over His house — whose house we are, if we hold fast our confidence and the outspokenness of our hope firm until the end. (Hebrews 3:6)

Yet Another Babylon

Not long past the end of the first century, Yahshua followed through on His warnings in the letters in Revelation to the churches: He spewed their lukewarm religion out of His mouth.[50] He came like a thief in the night and took away their lamp stands (the presence of His Spirit), and most of them didn't even notice.[51] The few overcomers died off,[52] and the rest went on with a form of religion that denied the power to love as they had in the beginning.[53] They had shifted off the rock they had been founded upon — the revelation that comes from obeying His commandments[54] — and as a result, darkness overtook them.[55]

In effect, spiritually they were carried off to Babylon. Their walls of protection had been breached because God could not hear their prayers over the clamor of their apostasy,[56] so the enemy came in like a flood and

---

[50] Revelation 3:16   [51] Revelation 3:3; 2:5; Romans 11:22   [52] Revelation 3:4
[53] 2 Timothy 3:5   [54] John 14:21; Matthew 7:24-27   [55] Matthew 16:17-18 (see *Upon this Rock* on page 43.   [56] *Apostasy* is departure from the apostles' teachings; see also *The Insurgent* on page 21 for more details on the condition of the church at the end of the first century. The following verses speak of what is required for one's prayers to be heard in heaven: 1 John 3:21-22; 1 Peter 3:12; Matthew 6:9-13; 1 Timothy 2:8

destroyed the Temple, stone by stone.[57] They were taken captive by the evil one to do his will.[58] But just as the Jews who were carried away to Babylon, they developed a whole new religion that did not depend on the Temple, that is, the corporeal[59] expression of the Body of Messiah — the daily laying down of their lives for one another,[60] the daily encouragement of their gatherings in which all prophesied,[61] and the visible unity and economic justice of their common life.[62]

This new religion followed the Nicolaitan (clergy/laity) pattern[63] rather than the earlier Judean (one heart and soul) pattern.[64] The people were content to just attend a "worship service" one day a week, in which nothing was expected of them but to follow a ritual of prescribed prayers, rote responses, and solemn hymns, and to hear a sermon prepared by the appointed (or self-appointed[65]) leader.

The apostle Paul had warned of the emergence of such a system, as the seeds of it had begun to germinate even while he was still alive:

> "I know that after my departure fierce wolves will come in among you, not sparing the flock; and from among your own selves will arise men speaking twisted things, to draw away the disciples after them. Therefore be alert..." (Acts 20:29-31)

> "For such men are false apostles, deceitful workmen, disguising themselves as apostles of Christ. And no wonder, for even Satan disguises himself as an angel of light. So it is no surprise if his servants, also, disguise themselves as servants of righteousness..." (2 Corinthians 11:13-15)

Messiah Himself, in His warnings to the churches, denounced these "synagogues of Satan"[66] that were beginning to appear as the first century was drawing to a close. Indeed, it was the exact counterpart of the synagogue system the leading Jews had developed in Babylon of old. They were led by those who claimed to be "Jews," but did not have the obedient heart, faith, or deeds of Abraham.[67] And of course, their gospel[68] was not the same gospel Abraham had obeyed, the one Yahshua had preached, that called everyone to forsake everything to follow Him. Instead, the new gospel made the many comfortable living their independent lives in "Babylon" while giving their offerings to support the

---

[57] 1 Peter 2:5   [58] 2 Timothy 2:26   [59] *Corporeal* means: 1) Having material or physical form or substance; 2) Affecting or characteristic of the body as opposed to the mind or spirit. Similar words for corporeal are the following: bodily, corporate, embodied, and incarnate.   [60] Luke 9:23; 1 John 3:16-17   [61] Hebrews 3:13; 10:24-25; 1 Corinthians 14:24-26   [62] John 17:21-23; Acts 4:32-35
[63] Revelation 2:6,15; the term *Nicolaitan* is derived from *nikao*, "to conquer," and *laos*, "people," hence, "people conquerors."   [64] Acts 4:32; 1 Thessalonians 2:14
[65] 3 John 1:9-10   [66] Revelation 2:9; 3:9   [67] Romans 2:29; Galatians 3:29; John 8:39; Matthew 3:9   [68] 2 Corinthians 11:4

few who became the clergy. The "litmus test" for the faith ceased to be the response of love and obedience that produced community,[69] but was replaced by "right doctrine" (as if the two could actually be separated).[70]

Of course, this new mystical religion came to be called *Christianity*. And just as Judaism developed in Babylon of old, Christianity became increasingly ritualistic and rigid, even centralizing its authority in a succession of popes analogous to the "Davidic dynasty" that the Jews had established in Babylon. Through its popes and bishops, Christianity repeatedly grabbed the reigns of the state to impose its will and to exact the support to feed its insatiable appetite for wealth and power, thus leaving a trail of blood stretching over 1,500 years. And lest anyone place the blame on the Roman Catholic Church alone, consider that her wayward daughters of the so-called Protestant Reformation exhibit the very same nature as their aged mother,[71] culminating in the utter confusion (*babel*) expressed in the 39,000+[72] divisions of Christianity today:

> And on her forehead was written a name of mystery: "Babylon the great, mother of prostitutes and of the abominations of the earth." (Revelation 17:5)

> "Fallen, fallen is Babylon the great! She has become a dwelling place for demons, a haunt for every unclean spirit, a haunt for every unclean bird, a haunt for every unclean and detestable beast. For all nations have drunk the wine of the passion of her immorality, and the kings of the earth have committed immorality with her, and the merchants of the earth have grown rich from the power of her luxurious living." (Revelation 18:2-4)

If you are a Christian, your soul is in great jeopardy. You have received a false gospel that has given you the false hope of going to heaven when you die. You have received another Jesus,[73] not the True One,[74] Yahshua the Messiah, therefore you are still in your sins. But if you are willing to do the Father's will, you can be released from your captivity, to serve Him where He is.[75] We invite you to come! ✣

> "Come out of her, My people, lest you take part in her sins, lest you share in her plagues; for her sins are heaped high as heaven, and God has remembered her iniquities." (Revelation 18:4-5)

---

[69] 1 John 3:14,16-18; 2:3-5   [70] See *The Paradigm Shift from Community to Doctrine* on page 135.   [71] See our book *The Black Box* for a more thorough treatment of this topic, available via our web site: *www.twelvetribes.org*   [72] "When Jesus said, 'Upon this rock I will build my church, and the gates of hell shall not prevail against it,' did he intend that those called to bear his name in the world would be divided into 39,000 competing denominations? That is the number of separate Christian bodies worldwide, according to missions statistician Todd Johnson of the World Christian Database." Timothy George, "Is Christ Divided?" *Christianity Today*, July, 2005.   [73] 2 Corinthians 11:4   [74] 1 John 5:20   [75] John 12:26

LEAVE

ENTER
BECOME

Abraham, c. 2000 BC

Thousands of years ago, God found a man who was completely willing to do His will. His heart was longing for something greater than the life he was living. Then one day he heard a voice speak something very clearly to his heart.

> *Now the LORD said to Abram, "Leave your country and your kindred and your father's house and go to the land that I will show you. And I will make of you a great nation, and I will bless you and make your name great, so that you will be a blessing. (Genesis 12:1-2)*

This man's name was Abram. At 75 years of age, he heard this call from God and he obeyed without hesitation.[1] He immediately left the land of his fathers, and after a long and difficult journey, he entered into the land that God showed him and became a new creation in the land of promise.[2] God called this new man *Abraham*, because he would be the father of a great nation, for God wanted a whole nation of people with the same heart as this man. Abraham's response to God's call would forever be the foundation for all those who would come after him, desiring to follow their Creator.[3]

Abraham was called to *leave* one place and *enter* into another. Had he not left the land of his fathers, he would not have been qualified to be the seed of the nation God wanted to establish. He had to obey the call. Some 4000 years later, the same response is required of anyone who wishes to be saved from this perverted generation.[4]

Babylon, c. 500 BC

Many years later, God called Abraham's wayward offspring, who had been in Babylon for 70 years of discipline, to leave and return to

---

[1] Genesis 12:4   [2] Genesis 17:1-8   [3] Hebrews 11:8; John 7:17-18   [4] Acts 2:40

Jerusalem and rebuild the temple.[5] Of the roughly one million Jews who were living in Babylon at that time, only about 42,000 returned.[6] Most had grown comfortable with their lives in Babylon. As Josephus, the first-century Jewish historian wrote in his chronicles, "…yet did many of them stay at Babylon, as not willing to leave their possessions."[7]

The journey back to Jerusalem was over 700 miles. It wasn't easy. The comforts of Babylon could not accompany those who left on the journey. But for those whose hearts were stirred by the call to return to the land that God had promised to their forefather Abraham, and to rebuild the temple in Jerusalem, the suffering could not compare with the joy set before them. It was only the remnant who thirsted for their land that heard the call and obeyed.

Galilee, c. 30 AD

These stories of Abraham, Israel, the Babylonian exile, and the return to rebuild were passed down from generation to generation until Yahshua[8] heard them from His mother and father, and from the rabbis. Surely, with His tender and pure heart, He must have asked His parents and teachers why so many stayed behind in Babylon. It must have been so difficult for Him to understand why anyone would not heed the call to return and rebuild their beloved city. Imagine the look on His young face when His parents had to explain to Him that it was because they had grown comfortable and didn't want to leave their possessions and unwilling family members. Why would anyone hesitate if their God was calling them? Why would anyone value *things* over doing God's will?

As time went by and Yahshua grew into a man, He found Himself extending the very same call to his fellow Israelites.[9]

> And Jesus, walking by the Sea of Galilee, saw two brothers, Simon called Peter, and Andrew his brother, casting a net into the sea; for they were fishermen. Then He said to them, "Follow Me, and I will make you fishers of men." They immediately left their nets and followed Him. Going on from there, He saw two other brothers, James the son of Zebedee, and John his brother, in the boat with Zebedee their father, mending their nets. He called them, and immediately they left the boat and their father, and followed Him." (Matthew 4:18-22)

> After that He went out and noticed a tax collector named Levi sitting in the tax booth, and He said to him, "Follow Me." And he left everything behind, and got up and began to follow Him." (Luke 5:27-28)

Yahshua called His disciples in the very same way that God had called both Abraham and the Jews out of Babylon. Those who were

---

[5] Ezra 1:3-5 [6] Ezra 2:64 [7] Josephus, *Antiquities of the Jews*, 11.1.1-3. [8] *Yahshua* is the Hebrew name of the Savior. See *The Name Above All Names*, p. 151. [9] Mark 1:16-20

stirred in their hearts did not hesitate, but left everything to follow him.[10] It was consistent with the way God had always called those who were willing to do His will.

However, like the many who had stayed behind in Babylon, there were many in the Master's day who chose comfort over their salvation. When a well-to-do young man came running and knelt down at Yahshua's feet, asking what he must do to gain eternal life, Yahshua answered,

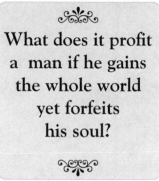

What does it profit a man if he gains the whole world yet forfeits his soul?

"Go your way, sell whatever you have and give to the poor, and you will have treasure in heaven; and come, take up your cross, and follow Me." (Mark 10:21)

Though the rich young man heard the clear call just as his forefather Abraham had, his face fell.[11] He valued his possessions more than following the Master. He had a *cause* to not obey Him.[12] The dark shadow of the torment he would someday face in death slowly fell over his face with the deepest gloom. He would rather have heard another message, one that would have allowed him to hold onto his life and possessions, but this was not the command, nor had it been for Abraham or the Jews in Babylon.

Peter, Andrew, James, and John left their nets,[13] which were their profession and livelihood, to follow the Master. Paul also "suffered the loss of all things,"[14] counting it as rubbish. All who responded to the gospel left everything behind. The contrast between Mark 10:28-30 and verses 17-22 is chilling. What does it profit a man if he gains the whole world yet forfeits his own soul?[15]

In the same manner as Abraham, those who heard the good news on the day of Pentecost, *gladly* received the message and left everything.[16] Their possessions were used to establish the first community, as it is recorded:

Now all who believed were together, and had all things in common, and sold their possessions and goods, and divided them among all, as anyone had need. (Acts 2:44-45; see also Acts 4:32-35)

So these steps are the steps of a faith that *works*. Abraham did it and started a whole new culture and nation. The first disciples did the same. Therefore, these same essential steps of *that* faith must be followed today

---

[10] Mark 10:28-30 [11] Mark 10:22 [12] Revelation 22:17 [13] Matthew 4:18-22
[14] Philippians 3:8 [15] Mark 8:36 [16] Acts 2:41

by anyone who desires to be saved.[17] All those in the first century who were cut to the heart by the gospel they heard knew what they had to do before they could call upon the name of the Lord to be saved. They understood that the terms of the gospel were life for life, without compromise. If they wanted to drink of the living water, it meant forsaking their life, and all that it encompassed, and being immersed into the new culture that was before them.

Here and Now

> *Then He said to me, "It is done. I am the Alpha and the Omega, the beginning and the end. I will give to the one who thirsts from the spring of the water of life without cost. He who overcomes will inherit these things, and I will be his God and he will be My son. But for the cowardly and unbelieving and abominable and murderers and immoral persons and sorcerers and idolaters and all liars, their part will be in the lake that burns with fire and brimstone, which is the second death." (Revelation 21:6-8)*

At the head of the list of those worthy of spending eternity in the lake of fire are the *cowardly and unbelieving*. They are those who, for the fear of losing their own life and possessions in this world, reject the gospel that they hear from a righteous sent one.[18] They do not overcome all that stands in the way of drinking the water of life. They are unwilling to leave their life in the fallen society. They have a cause that is greater in their eyes than the call of Messiah and His Bride:

> *"And the Spirit and the bride say, 'Come!' And the one who hears say, 'Come!' And let him who thirsts come. Whoever desires, let him take the water of life freely." (Revelation 22:17)*

---

[17] John 8:39   [18] Matthew 10:40-41; John 13:20; 7:17-18

The word translated *freely* literally means *without a cause* to hinder them from drinking. The word *come* means to leave one place and arrive at another.[19] So if anyone is truly *thirsty* for the water of eternal life, let him *overcome* anything that would hinder him, *leave* behind all that he possesses, and follow the Master in the same way the disciples did.[20] Those who are willing to do the will of the Father will *come* gladly, with great joy over the hope of gaining the thirst-quenching water of eternal life.[21]

The First Step in Obeying the Gospel

Just as Abraham and the disciples of old obeyed, the first step in obeying the gospel is to *leave* one place and *enter* another.[22] You leave your old life in this world and are born again into a brand new culture, with a brand new heart that is quenched of all thirst.[23] Abraham did what the rich young ruler would not do. He turned his back on his previous life. He did not cower back at the command to leave it all behind. He said his farewells, kissed his loved ones good-bye, and placed his life in the hands and care of the One who called him to the land of promise. None but the willing will *come* to this new place.

So can someone be a disciple, yet remain in Babylon? Can one become a disciple while remaining in his old life, at the same address, working the same job, enslaved to the same passions,[24] immersed in the affairs of this world?[25] Can one accept the world's values, judgments, and political pursuits and be a disciple?[26] Is it possible to wallow in the world's excesses, letting your children be trained by the world's standards and ideals,[27] being fully identified with the world, yet still claim to be following in the footsteps of Abraham?[28]

The answer is the same today as it was then: *No.*

---

[19] John 6:44 [20] Luke 10:16; Matthew 10:37; Luke 14:26,33 [21] Matthew 13:44
[22] Colossians 1:13; 1 Corinthians 1:2 — Paul was writing to those "in every place" (locality or township) who were set apart in communities where they were being sanctified (purified) through the refining fire of their common life, since "all who believed were together and shared all things in common" as in Acts 2:44. [23] Acts 5:20; 1 Corinthians 12:13; Acts 2:36-45 [24] 1 John 2:1 [25] 2 Timothy 2:4 [26] John 18:36 [27] In a recent poll of Christian families concerning how they raise their children, the top goal that parents had was their children getting a good education. Considering the words in Matthew 5:13-16, you may find the following quote surprising: "You might expect that parents who are born-again Christians would take a different approach to raising their children than did parents who have not committed their life to Christ, but that was rarely the case," Barna explained. "For instance, we found that the qualities born-again parents say an effective parent must possess, the outcomes they hope to facilitate in the lives of their children, and the media monitoring process in the household was indistinguishable from the approach taken by parents who are not born again." *Parents Describe How They Raise Their Children*, February 28, 2005, Barna Research Group. [28] 1 John 5:19

Leave, Enter, Become!

If you are willing to do the will of God, you will hear the call and come. You will *leave* your rotten, stinking life in this world and *enter* into the new life of love and forgiveness that the Messiah, Yahshua, is establishing in these last days.[29] Only *there* can you serve Him[30] by serving your brothers and sisters, night and day.[31] And only *there* can you *become* one of those whom He is not ashamed to call His brothers,[32] who together are being built into an eternal dwelling place for God by His Spirit.[33]

We welcome any who are still thirsty to come. ✻

---

[29] John 13:34-35   [30] John 12:26   [31] Acts 26:7   [32] Hebrews 2:11   [33] Ephesians 2:21-22; 4:16

> So Elijah departed from there and found Elisha
> the son of Shaphat, who was plowing with twelve yoke
> of oxen in front of him, and he was with the twelfth.
> Elijah passed by him and cast his cloak upon him.
> And he left the oxen and ran after Elijah and said,
> "Let me kiss my father and my mother,
> and then I will follow you."
> And he said to him, "Go and return to me,
> for what have I done to you?"
> And he returned from following him
> and took the yoke of oxen and sacrificed them
> and boiled their flesh with the yokes of the oxen
> and gave it to the people, and they ate.
> Then he arose and went after Elijah
> and served him.
> (1 Kings 19:19-21)

ELIJAH & ELISHA

According to 1 Kings 19:19-21, Luke 9:59-62, and Matthew 8:21-22, loyalty to Messiah must be first and foremost. He takes first place — preeminence over all other loyalties.[1] This is how our Master Yahshua,[2] the Messiah, trained and taught His disciples, and He told them to teach this to others.[3] This is clearly recorded in the Gospels, and is to be proclaimed to the whole world, indiscriminately.[4] The gospel makes the distinction between those who are willing to serve God and those who are not willing. It is the perfect test for all who hear it.[5] Yahshua's good news separates the sheep from the goats. It reveals the secret intentions of the

[1] Colossians 1:18 [2] *Yahshua* is the Hebrew name of the Savior; see *The Name Above All Names*, page 151. [3] Matthew 28:20 [4] John 7:17 [5] Matthew 7:21

hearer's heart.[6] It divides those who are willing to do the will of the Father from those who are not.[7]

Yahshua demanded that anyone He called into service as a disciple give his undivided attention to serving Him in the Community of the Redeemed as a member of His Body. As he said in Luke 9:62, "No one who puts his hand to the plow and turns back is fit for service in the kingdom of God.[8] To turn away from giving your undivided attention disqualifies you from the Kingdom of God in exactly the same way as a would-be disciple who does not want to obey the gospel is disqualified. Anything less than undivided attention is half-hearted discipleship. Divided loyalties make a person unfit for service in the kingdom of God.[9]

According to Ephesians 4:16, each part works together to build up Messiah's Body. This cannot be done back home, carrying on business as usual.[10] That's why Yahshua called His disciples to leave everything behind.[11] The demand of giving supreme loyalty to Messiah eliminates the "waste" or useless things from the Body. Anyone who is half-hearted will be disqualified[12] because he doesn't build up the Body. He is worthless as far as the kingdom is concerned, unfit for service. Half-hearted disciples will not enter the kingdom because they are not using all their talents.[13] They are not able to be used by their Master to the maximum,[14] thus they do not glorify the Father in heaven by bearing much fruit.[15]

There is no time for going back home and taking care of anything, which would consume your time and energy, preventing you from serving Yahshua to the utmost. The spiritually dead are to bury or take care of mother and father until they die.[16] Even though he forfeits his earthly inheritance, a disciple's loyalty to his Master Yahshua must be greater than his loyalty to his parents. This is another test to see whether someone's faith is genuine. Someone who obeys the gospel shows that he has genuine faith.[17]

Doing the Father's Business

Disciples have the urgent business of carrying out their fore-ordained works in the Body. This is their occupation. This is the reason they were chosen.[18] The master told his servants, "Do business until I return."[19] Even as a youth, Yahshua said, "Did you not know that I had to be in My Father's house, in His affairs, doing His business?"[20] By the time He was 12 years old, Yahshua had become a son of the commandment, a true *bar mitzvah*.[21] He had become responsible to keep the commandments. That's why He had gone to Jerusalem to that particular Passover feast. The Law

[6] Hebrews 4:12 [7] John 10:14,27-29 [8] Luke 14:26 [9] Luke 9:62 [10] Matthew 22:5; Revelation 19:9; Matthew 22:8 [11] Luke 14:26,33 [12] Matthew 13:48 [13] Matthew 25:30 [14] 1 Corinthians 3:12-15 [15] John 15:8 [16] Luke 9:60 [17] John 3:36 [18] Ephesians 1:4; 2:10; 4:12,16 [19] Luke 19:13 [20] Luke 2:49 [21] A *bar mitzvah* in fact, that is; the ritual use of the term in Judaism didn't come

required every male to appear three times a year before Yahweh in the place He had chosen for His name to dwell.[22] The Passover was one of those designated times.[23] So as a true *bar mitzvah* it was totally normal for Him to know that from then on He would engage in the affairs of His Father. Luke 2:50 indicates that His parents did not fully recognize the depth of this boy they were raising, and what they were raising Him for.

Whether you understand Luke 2:49 and the parable in Luke 19:11-27 or not depends on whether each is only a nice story to you rather than a revelation of one of the mysteries of the Kingdom of Heaven. Is your heart is dull or do you actually *understand* with your heart?[24]

Elijah's Mantle

Just as Elisha did greater works than Elijah, so Yahshua was also looking for someone who would do greater works than He.[25] Elijah threw his mantle on Elisha, designating, electing, or choosing one who was willing to do his will.[26] This signified that Elisha was to receive the authority and power of Elijah's anointing. 1 Kings 19:20-21 clearly reveals the ransom that Elisha had to give in order to follow Elijah. Elisha had to forsake his occupation, possessions, family, etc., for the sake of Yahweh and His word. Elisha broke with his past vocation, even as Yahshua's disciples left their nets and their fathers and mothers.[27]

After Elisha gave up his past life, his "business," he set out to follow Elijah as his attendant. Elisha became the disciple of Elijah, the one who served Elijah. The Hebrew word used in 1 Chronicles 15:2 is *sharat*. It means to wait on, to serve, to minister, to attend. Just as Yahshua said in John 12:25-26, to be His disciple, one must utterly forsake his former life, occupation, and location and serve the Master *where He is*. You cannot *attend* to His needs if you are not *with* Him. *Sharat* is the occupation of a disciple of Yahshua. That's what Yahshua meant when He said, "Go and make disciples."[28]

Unless you do exactly as Elisha did, leaving everything behind to be completely devoted, you cannot be Yahshua's attendant, minister, or disciple. Apart from doing this you do not have the *ability* to be a disciple of Yahshua. Luke 14:33 is the gospel you must practically obey. If not, you remain in God's wrath.[29] So the word *sharat* refers to the closest servants of Yahweh, who are *with* Him, carrying out His good pleasure.[30]

It was only after Elisha sacrificed all he had that he could follow Elijah as an attendant. Yahshua drew from this when He said in Luke 14:33, "If anyone wants to be My disciple he must 'kiss his old life good-bye.'" To "kiss your old life good-bye" is what Luke 14:26,33 and Mark

until much later. [22] Ezra 6:12; Exodus 34:23 [23] Deuteronomy 16:16 [24] Matthew 13:10-17 [25] John 14:12 [26] Isaiah 53:10-11; John 7:17; 1 Kings 19:16 [27] Matthew 4:20-22; Luke 14:26,33 [28] Luke 14:26-33; Matthew 28:19-20 [29] John 3:36 [30] Genesis 39:4; Exodus 33:11

10:28-30 are all about. 1 Kings 19:20 and Matthew 10:37-38 say the same thing. Elisha did both verses 37 and 38 to be worthy of Elijah.

Today in Christianity, the word *minister* amounts to the same as in 2 Corinthians 11:15 — a *minister of Satan*, which is only hucksterism in the eyes of those who are willing to do God's will.[31] Those who are willing know the difference between someone who is sent from God and someone who comes in his own authority.[32] If a person comes in his own authority, it permits Satan to put *his* mantle on him. The true meaning of the word *minister* has been maligned even as the name of God has by Christianity. In reality, the word *minister* implies discipleship, being yielded to the will of God, servanthood, and obedience to the gospel.

Elisha became Elijah's minister, servant, attendant, or disciple in training to take Elijah's place.[33] In 1 Kings 19:20, Elijah said "Go and return to me." Since he had already cast his mantle on Elisha, he could say, "Go and return to me, for I have *anointed* you; I have done something very important to you."[34] Elijah's approval to let Elisha kiss his parents good-bye was an indication of his assurance that Elisha had come under his anointing and authority. Elisha gave a farewell feast to his family. From then on he did not turn back from serving Elijah, just as Joshua was Moses' successor, attendant, and servant,[35] in contrast to what happened when Yahshua said virtually the same thing to the rich young ruler in Mark 10:21, "Go, sell everything you have... and come, follow Me."

To be Yahshua's *disciple* requires the very same devotion and loyalty as these attendants or disciples of the Old Covenant. This exactly is the meaning of what Yahshua commanded in Matthew 28:19-20, and of the many other words in Acts 2:37-41. The gospel brings you into discipleship, into total devotion and loyalty to Messiah, which causes His life to be made known.[36]

1 Kings 19:19-21 makes it absolutely clear that before Elisha could be Elijah's *disciple* or attendant he had to make the sacrifice — paying the *ransom*, as it were, with everything he had. This is where Yahshua got much of what He taught. He had only the Old Covenant scriptures to read and to draw from in order to form the new spiritual nation that would carry out the will of His heavenly Father here on earth. Until He sees the tangible fruit of that kingdom, He will not be satisfied, even 2,000 years later.[37]

Would the Son of God demand any less loyalty to His cause than Elijah? How then can we think we can be half-hearted? In Matthew 24:40-41, who was wholly devoted and who was half-hearted? ✳

---

[31] 2 Corinthians 2:17; John 7:17 [32] John 7:18 [33] 1 Kings 19:16-17; 19-21 [34] The *Complete Jewish Bible* gets the right sense of this verse: He left the oxen, ran after Eliyahu and said, *"Please let me kiss my father and mother good-bye; then I will follow you."* He answered, *"Go; but return, because of what I did to you."* [35] Exodus 24:13; 33:11; Deuteronomy 1:38; 3:38; 31:14; 34:9; Joshua 1:5 [36] Acts 2:44-45; 4:32,35 [37] Matthew 21:43; 24:14; 28:20; Isaiah 53:11

THE GOLDEN CALF, THE GOSPEL, AND THE ROYAL PRIESTHOOD

The gospel proclaimed by Yahshua, the Messiah, was a radical message that cut right to the core of what separated man from His Creator. Those who received His message were bound together in a radically committed life, which demonstrated Yahshua's victory over the power of sin and death. Yahshua's gospel was not something He came up with on His own, but was consistent with the demand that God has always made on those who would serve Him — complete loyalty and devotion. So to really understand the gospel in its fullness, one must understand the history of God's dealings with man.

There is a very significant and heartbreaking story in the Old Testament that few Christians even know, and fewer still understand, though its message is the very foundation of the Gospel. It is the story of the fall of Israel from its original calling to be a whole kingdom of priests, not just one tribe of priests and eleven tribes of laymen. Here is what Yahweh, the God of Israel, spoke through Moses to the entire twelve tribes after they came out of Egypt, and their response:

> *"Now therefore, if you will indeed obey My voice and keep My covenant, you shall be My treasured possession among all peoples, for all the earth is Mine; and you shall be to Me a kingdom of priests and a holy nation. These are the words that you shall speak to the people of Israel." So Moses came and called the elders of the people and set before them all these words that Yahweh had commanded him. All the people answered together and said, "All that Yahweh has spoken we will do." And Moses reported the words of the people to Yahweh. (Exodus 19:5-8)*

God's deep desire for Israel was that they would be a shining light amongst all the nations around them. He wanted them be a witness to the nations of what He is like by their unity as a commonwealth of twelve tribes, and by their life of righteousness and justice.[1] For that is what it means to be a priest, and to be a priesthood: to represent God's heart and nature to man, not only in word, but also in how they live before the nations around them. They stand between God and man, reconciling man to his Maker. But if they compromise their priesthood by giving their affection to other gods, they forfeit their priesthood, for they no longer represent the one true God. Without a priesthood there is no way for man to be reconciled to God.

Tragically, that is exactly what happened with Israel not long after they vowed to be God's holy priesthood. The poignant story is told in Exodus 32. Moses had gone up on Mt. Sinai to hear from Yahweh, who had miraculously delivered them from the oppression they were under in Egypt. There he received the Ten Commandments on tablets of stone, but he was gone for longer than the people expected. In their restless anxiety, thinking Moses to have perished on the mountain, they pressured Aaron to make them a god to worship. It was going to take a lot to win their hearts back from the idolatry and sensual worship they had been immersed in for generations in Egypt.

Seeing their waywardness, Yahweh sent Moses down the mountain to deal with his people. Moses found the Israelites dancing around a golden calf, having totally abandoned themselves to their idolatry. Amazingly, Moses expressed God's great mercy by giving them another chance to respond to His call:

> When Moses saw that the people were running wild (for Aaron had let them run wild, to the derision of their enemies), then Moses stood in the gate of the camp, and said, "Who is on Yahweh's side? Come to me!" And all the sons of Levi gathered around him.
>
> He said to them, "Thus says Yahweh, the God of Israel, 'Put your sword on your side, each of you! Go back and forth from gate to gate throughout the camp, and each of you kill your brother, your friend, and your neighbor.'" The sons of Levi did as Moses commanded, and about three thousand of the people fell on that day.
>
> Moses said, "Today you have ordained yourselves for the service of Yahweh, each one at the cost of a son or a brother, and so have brought a blessing on yourselves this day." (Exodus 32:25-29)

Sadly, only the Levites responded to the call to serve Yahweh — but not all of them. Therefore those who responded were commanded to take their swords and kill their fellow tribesmen who were not willing to

---

[1] Genesis 18:19; Isaiah 5:7

Today you have ordained yourselves for the service of Yahweh, each one at the cost of a son or a brother...

forsake their idolatry. Thus the tribe of Levi was cleansed that day, and those who remained became Yahweh's holy priesthood. They had "ordained themselves" to this priesthood at the cost of their unwilling kinsmen. Otherwise their pleasure-loving, idolatrous kinsmen would have defiled the last remnant of true devotion in Israel.

Speaking of this pivotal event in the history of Israel, Moses later writes:

> At that time Yahweh set apart the tribe of Levi to carry the ark of the covenant of Yahweh to stand before Yahweh to minister to him and to bless his name, to this day. Therefore Levi has no portion or inheritance with his brothers. Yahweh is his inheritance, as Yahweh your God said to him. (Deuteronomy 10:8-9)

The Life of the Royal Priesthood

Not only did the Levites have to totally forsake their unwilling relatives, but they also forfeited any personal material wealth they could have claimed in the land, for they would live a life of total devotion to Yahweh. He saw fit to gather them into priestly "cities" where they would be utterly dependent upon Him to provide for them:

> Command the people of Israel to give to the Levites some of the inheritance of their possession as cities for them to dwell in. And you shall give to the Levites pasture lands around the cities. The cities shall be theirs to dwell in, and their pasture lands shall be for their cattle and for their livestock and for all their beasts. (Numbers 35:2-3)

These priestly "cities" were not as one would think of a city today. They were actually small walled villages about two-thirds of a mile in diameter, with a narrow band of shared pasture land around them.[2] Within those walls the Levites lived together as a close-knit community,

---

[2] Numbers 35:4-5

working together on their shared lands for their common good. Each of the men had allotted times when they would serve in the Temple in Jerusalem,[3] knowing that their wives and children would be well cared for back home in their priestly communities.

The Levitical priesthood was a type or foreshadow of what the New Covenant priesthood would be like, from the radical manner of their calling to their set-apart life and their ministry in the Temple. As the Apostle Peter wrote to the early church, taking Exodus 19:6 and applying it directly to them:

> But you are a chosen race, a royal priesthood, a holy nation, a people for his own possession, that you may proclaim the excellencies of him who called you out of darkness into his marvelous light. (1 Peter 2:9)

Indeed, they were "called out of darkness" to be His holy priesthood just as decisively as the Levites were called out of the idolatry that Israel had fallen into in Exodus 32. It is no mere coincidence that the Master's words echo the words of Moses:

> "Whoever is not with Me is against Me, and whoever does not gather with Me scatters." (Matthew 12:30)

> "Do not think that I have come to bring peace to the earth. I have not come to bring peace, but a sword. For I have come to set a man against his father, and a daughter against her mother, and a daughter-in-law against her mother-in-law. And a person's enemies will be those of his own household. Whoever loves father or mother more than Me is not worthy of Me, and whoever loves son or daughter more than Me is not worthy of Me." (Matthew 10:34-37)

> "If anyone comes to Me and does not hate his own father and mother and wife and children and brothers and sisters, yes, and even his own life, he cannot be My disciple… Likewise, whoever of you does not forsake all that he has cannot be My disciple." (Luke 14:26,33)

Yahshua's Obedience to the Gospel

Yahshua did not call His followers to literally kill their unwilling relatives, but He did call them to sever their ties to their former lives, including unwilling family and friends,[4] and be immersed into a new spiritual family. As an example to all who would follow Him, Yahshua cut off the influence of His own mother and brothers when they sought to restrain His "madness"[5]:

> And the crowd came together again, so that they could not even eat. When His family heard it, they went out to restrain Him, for people were saying,

---

[3] 1 Chronicles 9:25; 24:19; Luke 1:23   [4] Matthew 4:18-22; Mark 10:28   [5] Mark 3:20-21

> *"He has gone out of his mind." ... Then His mother and His brothers came; and standing outside, they sent to Him and called Him. A crowd was sitting around Him; and they said to Him, "Your mother and your brothers are outside, asking for you." And He replied, "Who are My mother and My brothers?" And looking at those who sat around Him, He said, "Here are My mother and My brothers! Whoever does the will of God is My brother and sister and mother." (Mark 3:20,21,31-35)*

This was the "sword" that pierced Mary's heart, in fulfillment of the prophecy of Simeon at Yahshua's dedication in the Temple:

> *Then Simeon blessed them and said to His mother Mary, "This child is destined for the falling and the rising of many in Israel, and to be a sign that will be opposed so that the inner thoughts of many will be revealed — and a sword will pierce your own soul too." (Luke 2:34-35)*

That sword did its work, as Yahshua's mother and brothers were evidently cut to the heart by His words that day, and later were numbered among His disciples. Others wanted to follow Him conditionally, but His command was as clear as that of Moses:

The Cost of Following Yahshua

> *To another He said, "Follow me." But he said, "Lord, let me first go and bury my father." And Jesus said to him, "Leave the dead to bury their own dead. But as for you, go and proclaim the kingdom of God."*
>
> *Yet another said, "I will follow You, Lord, but let me first say farewell to those at my home." Jesus said to him, "No one who puts his hand to the plow and looks back is fit for the kingdom of God." (Luke 9:59-62)*

And perhaps the most well-known example is that of the "Rich Young Ruler" who came running after Yahshua and asked, "What must I do to inherit eternal life?" The Master's command was clear:

> *"You lack one thing: go, sell all that you have and give to the poor, and you will have treasure in heaven; and come, follow Me." Disheartened by the saying, he went away sorrowful, for he had great possessions. (Mark 10:21-22)*

Many Christians would say, "That was only for him, since he was so attached to his possessions." Even Yahshua's disciples were surprised, perhaps because they had been poor and hadn't had so much materially to leave behind, but the Master was calling even the rich to abandon their riches. Peter spoke for them all, and the Master's response made the "Good News" crystal clear:

> *Then Peter began to say to Him, "See, we have left all and followed You." So Jesus answered and said, "Assuredly, I say to you, there is no one who*

has left house or brothers or sisters or father or mother or wife or children or lands, for My sake and the gospel's, who shall not receive a hundredfold now in this time — houses and brothers and sisters and mothers and children and lands, with persecutions — and in the age to come, eternal life." (Mark 10:28-30, NKJ)

Yahshua did not envision just a little rag-tag band of disciples such as they were then, but a spiritual nation bursting forth from the hundredfold increase that would result from each disciple's unconditional surrender of his life and possessions — for Yahshua's sake and the gospel's sake. He envisioned nothing less than the "priestly cities" of the New Covenant holy priesthood — communities of disciples sharing a common, set-apart life together as a light to the perverse society around them.

The Restoration of the Twelve Tribes of Israel

It was not "out of the blue" that Yahshua had told His disciples, "You are the light of the world. A city set on a hill cannot be hidden."[6] And it was not a mere coincidence that He chose *twelve* apostles to pour this vision into, for He had in mind the restoration of the twelve-tribed royal priesthood that Israel was supposed to be.[7] But this time it would be tribes of a common *spiritual* stock, not necessarily the same physical bloodline. It would be the extended family of those who *do* the will of God.[8] Their priestly "cities" (communities) would be filled with grateful disciples who love one another just as He loved them,[9] who daily lay down their lives for one another,[10] and who daily encourage one another,[11] continually making sure that no one is falling short of the grace of God.[12]

Yahshua's apostles clearly took on both His gospel and His vision, for when the Holy Spirit came upon them on the day of Pentecost, that gospel is what they spoke with much passion, as is evident from the results of their preaching. In the same spirit of Moses and Yahshua, Peter exhorted the people, "Be saved from this perverse generation!" And 3,000 people responded by forsaking everything and banding together as a spiritual brotherhood:

Now all who believed were together, and had all things in common, and sold their possessions and goods, and divided them among all, as anyone had need. So continuing daily with one accord in the temple, and breaking bread from house to house, they ate their food with gladness and simplicity of heart. (Acts 2:44-46)

Now the full number of those who believed were of one heart and soul, and no one said that any of the things that belonged to him was his own, but they had all things in common. And with great power the apostles were

---

[6] Matthew 5:14   [7] Exodus 19:5-6; 1 Peter 2:9-10; Isaiah 49:6   [8] Mark 3:34-34
[9] John 13:34-35   [10] 1 John 3:16   [11] Hebrews 3:13   [12] Hebrews 12:15

giving witness to the resurrection of the Lord Jesus, and abundant grace was upon them all. There was not a needy person among them, for as many as were owners of lands or houses sold them and brought the proceeds of what was sold and laid it at the apostles' feet, and it was distributed to each as any had need. (Acts 4:32-35)

This vibrant community would be the first of many priestly communities established all over Judea according to the same pattern as the community in Jerusalem, and then throughout the Mediterranean world.[13] Within about 30 years, the Apostle Paul was able to describe this emerging holy nation as "our twelve tribes who earnestly serve God night and day"[14] — His New Covenant royal priesthood. The apostles frequently exhorted the communities to be faithful in their priestly service:

> **It was not a mere coincidence that Yahshua chose twelve apostles to pour His vision into, for He had in mind the restoration of the twelve-tribed royal priesthood that Israel was supposed to be.**

You yourselves like living stones are being built up as a spiritual house, to be a holy priesthood, to offer spiritual sacrifices acceptable to God through Jesus Christ. (1 Peter 2:5)

Therefore I exhort first of all that supplications, prayers, intercessions, and giving of thanks be made for all men, for kings and all who are in authority, that we may lead a quiet and peaceable life in all godliness and reverence... I desire then that in every place the men should pray, lifting holy hands without wrath or dissension... (1 Timothy 2:1,2,8)

I beseech you therefore, brethren, by the mercies of God, that you present your bodies a living sacrifice, holy, acceptable to God, which is your reasonable [priestly] service. (Romans 12:1)

The Demise of the First-Century Church

But the very strength of Paul's exhortations is an indication that the church was already in decline in the latter part of the first century. Indeed, there are many indications in the apostles' letters that the church was losing its set-apart, priestly way of life, and falling back into the ways of the world around them.[15] By the end of the first century, Yahshua

---

[13] 1 Thessalonians 2:14; Acts 1:8 [14] Acts 26:7 [15] For example: 2 Timothy 2:4; 1 Corinthians 3:16-17; 2 Corinthians 6:14-18; 11:3-4; 1 John 5:21

Himself wrote to the church through the Apostle John:

> *"But I have this against you, that you have abandoned the love you had at first. Remember therefore from where you have fallen; repent, and do the works you did at first. If not, I will come to you and remove your lampstand from its place, unless you repent."* *(Revelation 2:4-5)*

Yahshua warned of the impending judgment that was coming upon the early church. The loss of their "lampstand" was tantamount to the loss of their priesthood, for they ceased receiving the illumination of the Holy Spirit and became as natural men, incapable of being a light to the surrounding darkness. Woefully, not long into the second century, that darkness consumed them,[16] as is evident from the apostate condition of the church described in the letter of James,[17] chronologically the last letter of the New Testament.

Bloody Church History

Gone were the priestly communities of outspoken disciples[18] consumed with a fervent love for one another that had caused their lives to be knit together into holy commonwealth,[19] which Paul had once been so bold as to call "The Israel of God."[20] They were replaced by what Yahshua Himself called "Synagogues of Satan,"[21] where a lukewarm[22] and silent laity[23] were presided over by supposed ministers of righteousness who were in fact Satan's servants.[24] Ironically, these "Nicolaitans"[25] soon came to be called priests, and indeed they were, but not for Yahweh, the

---

[16] John 9:4   [17] See *The Insurgent* on page 21.   [18] 1 Corinthians 14:26; Hebrews 3:6
[19] Ephesians 2:12   [20] Galatians 6:16   [21] Revelation 2:9; 3:9   [22] Revelation 3:16
[23] *Laity* — In Christianity, members of the religion that do not have the priestly responsibilities of ordained clergy.   [24] 2 Corinthians 11:14-15   [25] Revelation 2:6,15 — The word *Nicolaitan* is derived from *nikao*, meaning "to conquer," and *laos*, meaning "people," hence, "people conquerors" — the clergy who do all the speaking for the silent laity. For more on this subject see *The Incumbency*, page 45.

God of Israel. He could not hear their prayers over the discordant noise of their divided and soon-to-be warring factions.[26]

1900 years of discord, persecution, murder, genocide, immorality and injustice among Christians have come and gone since the first-century church fell from its priesthood. Today there are some 39,000 Christian denominations[27] that abundantly fulfill the prophetic words of the Apostle Paul in 2 Timothy 3:1-5, having the appearance of godliness but lacking the power to live a priestly life together in love and unity. They are far from bearing the fruit of the Kingdom which Yahshua longed for when He pronounced old Israel cut off from its holy root:

> *"Therefore I say to you, the kingdom of God will be taken from you and given to a nation bearing the fruits of it." (Matthew 21:43)*

The fruitless branches of Christianity are merely the tragic evidence that Paul's warning to the early church went unheeded:

> *For if God did not spare the natural branches, neither will He spare you. Therefore consider the goodness and severity of God: on those who fell, severity; but toward you, goodness, if you continue in His goodness. Otherwise you also will be cut off. (Romans 11:21-22)*

The Restoration of Israel in these Last Days

The good news is that in these last days a little sprig has sprouted from the ancient and holy root of the "olive tree" Paul spoke of.[28] It is growing into a new spiritual Israel of twelve tribes, a holy priesthood that is again earnestly serving God night and day for the hope of His promise to Abraham.[29] We live together in communities in twelve geographic regions around the world, striving to love one another and guard our unity with great diligence. We have forsaken everything to be grafted into this life, just as did the disciples of old. And we are earnestly searching for all of our brothers and sisters who are still lost in the confusion of Christianity and Judaism, and the futility of their independent lives in this fallen world, but who are willing to do our Father's will. Perhaps you are one of them. ✤

> *And the Spirit and the bride say, "Come!" And let him who hears say, "Come!" And let him who thirsts come. Whoever desires, let him take the water of life freely.[30] (Revelation 22:17)*

[26] 1 Timothy 2:8; Galatians 5:15; James 4:1-2 [27] *International Bulletin of Missionary Research*, Vol. 31, No. 1, p. 8. [28] Romans 11:17; Job 14:7-9 [29] Acts 26:7; Revelation 21:9,12 [30] The word *freely* here means without any cause to hold back from drinking deeply.

THE END OF DEATH'S REIGN

"Yet death reigned from Adam to Moses..."
(Romans 5:14)

The cold grip of death tugs relentlessly at the soul of every man, no matter how lofty his ideals, as if to claim its fair wages in advance of his dying breath. The evil ruler of the unseen realm knows the Bible all too well. Eager to exact the justice due him, he plays with the sin-sick souls of men as a cat plays with a mouse, holding them captive to the fear of death. For some, depression works best, for others, a manic denial of their sorry circumstances, or an unbridled obsession for sex, or money, or recognition — anything to capture the soul, crush the spirit, and silence the objective voice of man's conscience. Thus Satan feeds his insatiable desire for the destruction of God's image in man.

Yes, it is true: All men sin,[1] and the wages of sin is death,[2] therefore it is appointed to man to die once, and then comes the Judgment.[3] And yes, it is also true that the Messiah was offered once to bear the sins of many,[4] and set them free from their captivity to the evil ruler of this world.[5] So who are the "many" whose sins He bore? "But," you may object, "He bore the sins of the whole world!" And so it may seem from a casual reading of this popular verse:

---

[1] Romans 5:12 [2] Romans 6:23 [3] Hebrews 9:27 [4] Hebrews 9:28
[5] Colossians 1:13; Romans 6:6-7; John 8:36

He is the atoning sacrifice for our sins, and not only for ours, but also for the sins of the whole world. (1 John 2:22)

But obviously the whole world is not experiencing freedom from Satan's reign — not even the many who claim Christ as their Savior. Statistics consistently show that Christians in America are as much in the grip of the world's vices as the unbelieving society in which they are immersed.[6] How then can they claim to be saved from sin's dominion? For the Apostle Paul wrote of the profound effect *in this life* of having received the benefit of Messiah's sacrificial death:

*For if, by the trespass of the one man, death reigned through that one man, **how much more** will those who receive God's abundant provision of grace and of the gift of righteousness **reign in life** through the one man, Jesus Christ. (Romans 5:17)*

So whoever is still a slave to sin has obviously not received God's abundant provision of grace through Messiah's sacrifice, or His gift of righteousness, regardless of what he claims to believe.[7] Clearly something more than that kind of belief[8] is required on the part of the sinner in order for his sins to be borne by the Savior, releasing him from his slavery to sin.

Perhaps the key to understanding what is required can be found in the puzzling statement that Paul began his thought with a few verses back: "Yet death reigned from Adam to Moses…"[9] Why didn't he say, "Yet death reigned from Adam to *Christ*"? What did Moses do to bring an end to death's reign? Well, it was through Moses that God gave the law, the priesthood, and the sacrificial system, and through these He provided a way for a man's sins to be atoned for, loosening death's grip on his soul. If we can understand how this sacrificial system worked, then maybe we can understand why Christianity today doesn't work — and where to find the faith that works.

---

[6] Depression, and the taking of antidepressants, is as pervasive among Christians as in the broader society. And according to The Barna Group (www.barna.org), a conservative Christian research agency, the divorce rate among Christians in America is the same as that among non-Christians. One Barna project director admitted, *"We have found that in a lot of ways Christians are not living different lives than non-Christians, when we look at their behavior… It's hard for Christians to understand because it seems contrary to what people think would happen…We would love to be able to report that Christians are living very distinct lives and impacting the community, but … in the area of divorce rates they continue to be the same."* (John Rossomando, "Born-Again Christians No More Immune to Divorce than Others, Says Author," CNSNews.com, January 21, 2002) Barna also reports that there is no difference between "born-again" and unchurched adults in the likelihood of viewing pornography on the Internet, or reading magazines or watching videos with explicit sexual content.   [7] Romans 6:16-18   [8] John 2:23-25   [9] Romans 5:13

It has been said of old Israel's animal sacrifices that enough blood was shed to float a battleship.[10] If even a sparrow doesn't fall to the ground without our Father taking notice,[11] how much more did He care about the lifeblood of all those animals that served

His people? Was it all poured out in vain? The writer of Hebrews taught that without the shedding of blood, there is no forgiveness of sin,[12] yet it is impossible for the blood of bulls and goats to take away sins.[13] So why did the Law require animal sacrifices? The key is found in what happened in a sensitive human heart during the shedding of that blood.

The Sin Offering

This was the law of the sin offering for a common Israelite:

> *If anyone of the common people sins unintentionally in doing any one of the things that by the LORD's commandments ought not to be done, and realizes his guilt, or the sin which he has committed is made known to him, he shall bring for his offering a goat, a female without blemish, for his sin which he has committed. And he shall lay his hand on the head of the sin offering and kill the sin offering in the place of burnt offering. And the priest shall take some of its blood with his finger and put it on the horns of the altar of burnt offering and pour out all the rest of its blood at the base of the altar… Thus the priest shall make atonement for him, and he shall be forgiven.* (Leviticus 4:27-31)

Unless you happen to be a goat farmer, it will be very hard for you to put yourself in the place of this Israelite of old who must offer a sacrifice for his sin — a perfect female goat from his herd. Notice that it says *female*. It would have been easier if it had said *male*, for you don't get so personally attached to the bucks. You keep a few on hand for breeding, but you don't handle them so much. The extras you kill for meat. But it's the *females* that receive your tender care, for they are the most valuable. They provide milk to feed your family, and they bear kids every spring.

---

[10] For a small battleship of 10,000 tons, that would require over two million gallons of blood. [11] Matthew 10:29 [12] Hebrews 9:22 [13] Hebrews 10:4

And it's the ones without blemish that you value the most, not only because you want to increase your herd with their offspring, but also because they win your heart.

So there you are, an Israelite who has become conscious of your sin, because the Law has done its work of identifying your transgressions.[14] Perhaps you try to push it out of your mind for a time, but eventually the guilt of your sin weighs heavily upon you. Looking over your herd of goats, you pick out the yearlings[15] from among the females. They are so sweet and innocent. Knowing already which one is your favorite, you find yourself trying to justify choosing one of the other nice goats, which you reason would also be considered "without blemish" in anyone else's eyes. The priest wouldn't know the difference, but you would, and your God would. You would just be fooling yourself if you didn't offer your best. Your sacrifice would not be acceptable, and your sins would not be forgiven.

So taking your best yearling doe, you head out on the familiar but difficult path to Jerusalem to present yourself to the priest at the Temple. Along the way, the goat's innocent bleating causes you to grieve over your sin and the death it produces, taking its toll in your own life, and prematurely ending the life of this beautiful animal. All too soon you find yourself at the Temple. Kneeling in front of the altar of burnt offerings and laying your hands gently on the head of the goat as the priest restrains it, you confess your sins in the simple faith that God will transfer your guilt to that innocent animal. Then the priest takes a razor-sharp knife and slits the animal's throat, and you watch helplessly as its lifeblood spurts into the waiting basin with each beat of its heart, until the goat collapses in its last spasm of death. The priest pours its blood out at the base of the altar, and tells you that your sin is forgiven. You realize that your heart is pounding more than the goat's was, and as you walk away, the cost of your forgiveness causes you to cry out to your God to help you overcome the sin that keeps bringing you back to this place.

Was the guilt actually borne by the goat? Of course not. A goat is not a moral creature with an eternal soul that can bear guilt. But the goat, as an innocent and unblemished sacrifice, was a *type* or foreshadow of the One who was to come. He would indeed bear the sins of all whose faith was expressed in giving their best in obedience and childlike trust, along with the sincere and complete confession of their sins. Our Father, seeing the honest and sincere heart of the offerer, covered his sins until the time when Messiah would come to give His life as the culmination of all the sacrifices offered in sincerity, and to release these captives waiting in "Abraham's bosom."[16]

---

[14] Romans 3:20; 5:13; 7:7   [15] Numbers 15:27   [16] Luke 16:22; Ephesians 4:8

The Scapegoat

The sacrifice for personal sins was not the only type that looked forward to Messiah. Each year on the Day of Atonement, two male goats were chosen for a special kind of sin offering — for the sins of the whole nation. The high priest would kill the first goat in the customary way for a sin offering, but the second goat he presented live:

And Aaron shall lay both his hands on the head of the live goat, and confess over it all the iniquities of the people of Israel, and all their transgressions, all their sins. And he shall put them on the head of the goat and send it away into the wilderness by the hand of a man who is in readiness. The goat shall bear all their iniquities on itself to a remote area, and he shall let the goat go free in the wilderness. (Leviticus 16:21-22)

This is where the term *scapegoat* comes from. It became the custom in Israel that when the second goat was released, all the people would curse it, hurling insults, derision, and scorn upon the poor animal as it fled the angry mob, only to meet certain death by wild animals in the wilderness. It is not hard to see how this goat also foreshadowed what would happen to Messiah at the hands of His own countrymen:

But one of them, Caiaphas, who was high priest that year, said to them, "You know nothing at all. Nor do you understand that it is better for you that one man should die for the people, not that the whole nation should perish." He did not say this of his own accord, but being high priest that year he prophesied that Jesus would die for the nation. (John 11:49-51)

Just as happened to that innocent scapegoat, the Jews heaped their scorn and derision upon the innocent man, Yahshua, the Messiah sent to save them. They cursed Him and spat upon Him and treated Him shamefully, driving Him outside the gates of Jerusalem to the certain death that awaited Him. Little did they know, they were fulfilling the prophetic significance of all those poor scapegoats that gave up their lives for the nation each year on the Day of Atonement.

The Passover Lamb

But probably the most familiar Old Testament foreshadow of Messiah's sacrifice is the offering of the Passover lamb, to which the Apostle Paul makes explicit reference:

> *Christ, our Passover lamb, has been sacrificed. Let us therefore celebrate the festival, not with the old leaven, the leaven of malice and evil, but with the unleavened bread of sincerity and truth. (1 Corinthians 5:7-8)*

Indeed, according to John's Gospel, Yahshua died on the cross at the same time as the Jews were killing their Passover lambs,[17] and ironically, the chief priests petitioned Pilate to break His legs so that He would die[18] and be taken down from the cross before evening, so as not to defile their ritual observance of the Passover.[19] But He had already died from the crushing weight of our sins which cut Him off from His Father,[20] so it was not necessary to break His legs, even as a Passover lamb's bones were not to be broken.[21]

For the Israelites of old, the Passover lamb was an expression of their utter trust and dependency upon the God of Israel to deliver them from death. On the 10th day of the first month,[22] each household was to take from their flock their best yearling male lamb, one without blemish, and "keep" it close to them until the 14th day:[23]

> *…and you shall keep it until the fourteenth day of this month, when the whole assembly of the congregation of Israel shall kill their lambs at twilight. (Exodus 12:6)*

---

[17] John 19:14; Exodus 12:6 [18] A person being crucified was unable to breathe unless he could push himself up with his legs, taking the strain off his chest. [19] John 19:31 [20] Matthew 27:46,50; Isaiah 53:10-11 [21] John 19:36; Exodus 12:46 [22] That is, the first month of the Hebrew calendar, which was the beginning of spring. [23] Exodus 12:3-6

The Hebrew word translated as "keep" in this verse is translated as "become" or "come to be" almost everywhere else it is used in the Old Testament. The implication was that they would become very attached to this sweet lamb so that they would really suffer to take its life at the end of that 14th day. In tears they would put its blood on the door posts and lintel of their house, and eat its roasted flesh with bitter herbs safe inside their house, trusting that the death angel would see the blood and pass over them.[24]

> The blood shall be a sign for you, on the houses where you are. And when I see the blood, I will pass over you, and no plague will befall you to destroy you, when I strike the land of Egypt. (Exodus 12:13)

Their deliverance from the slow death of bondage in Egypt and the immediate death of their firstborn offspring would not come without shedding the blood of an innocent animal. On the scale of things, it was a small price to pay for their freedom, but in order for it to be acceptable and effectual it required their utter sincerity and unflinching obedience. Any who failed to choose their best lamb, or failed to let their heart pity it, also failed to receive the salvation they tried to weasel out of God, for God is not mocked.[25]

Shut the Doors!

Over 400 years before the Messiah walked the dusty roads of Palestine, the prophet Malachi cried out to the backsliding nation of Israel,

> "When you offer blind animals in sacrifice, is that not evil? And when you offer those that are lame or sick, is that not evil? Present that to your governor; will he accept it or show you favor?" says the LORD of hosts… "Oh that there were one among you who would shut the doors, that you might not kindle fire on my altar in vain! I have no pleasure in you," says the LORD of hosts, "and I will not accept an offering from your hand." (Malachi 1:8,10)

After Malachi's death, no prophetic voice was heard in Israel until the days of John the Baptist, four centuries later. Although the Levitical priesthood continued to go through the motions of offering the ritual sacrifices in the Temple, most of that blood was shed in vain. But finally, in the fullness of time, our Father found a handful of sincere Israelites who were looking for the consolation of Israel, longing for the promised Messiah to come and deliver them from their bondage.

Through a miracle conceived in the heart of God before time began, a poor Hebrew virgin named Miriam[26] became pregnant and gave birth to

---

[24] Exodus 12:7-8   [25] Galatians 6:7   [26] Or *Mary* in English.

a child whom she was told to call *Yahshua*, which means "Yahweh's Salvation," for He would save His people from their sins.[27] He was the "only begotten" Son of God in that the seed that caused conception in Miriam's womb was a pure human seed preserved by God from before the Fall, not the fallen seed of Adam through her betrothed husband Yoceph.[28] Therefore Yahshua did not inherit the sin nature common to all who are descended from Adam.

The Lamb of God

When John the Baptist first saw Yahshua coming down to the Jordan River, the Holy Spirit spoke through him the prophetic words, "Behold, the Lamb of God, who takes away the sin of the world!"[29] Those words would echo in the minds of sensitive ones who witnessed the willing sacrifice of His life on the cross only a few years later. Indeed, this man, Yahshua of Nazareth, was to be the fulfillment of all the sacrifices offered in faith by sincere Israelites since the Law was given through Moses.

Not only was Yahshua born without blemish, but He lived His entire life in unbroken communion with His Father in heaven, doing all the Father's will, not once succumbing to any temptation. He never took a thought for Himself, but instead was always concerned for others, loving even those who hated Him, even to His dying breath. That is why the Father loved Him so much.[30] He was the very best that the Father had to give, which is why the most famous verse in the Bible is so significant:

For God so loved the world that He gave His only begotten Son, that whoever believes in Him should not perish but have everlasting life. (John 3:16)

God did not expect His people to do what He was unwilling to do Himself, therefore He did not withhold His very best — His beloved, only begotten Son with whom He had sweet communion — but gave Him to be slain as a sacrifice for our sins.

Like all the sacrifices sincerely offered before Him, Yahshua was an innocent lamb without blemish, but unlike all those sacrifices, He had a human soul that could actually bear the guilt of all who would "lay their hands" on Him. Therefore, in the last moments of His life, the guilt of all the sins that had been confessed by sincere Israelites as they laid their hands on the heads of their sacrificial lambs was placed upon Him, along with the guilt of all the sins confessed by His true disciples up until the day of His return. He literally *became* our sin,[31] and His Father, from whom Yahshua had never experienced one moment's separation, turned away from Him.[32]

---

[27] Matthew 1:21 [28] Or *Joseph* in English. [29] John 1:29 [30] John 10:17; Mark 1:11 [31] 2 Corinthians 5:21; Isaiah 53:4-12 [32] Matthew 27:46; Mark 15:34

It was the weight of our sins and the separation from His Father that finally snuffed out His life, not the excruciating physical suffering on the cross. Although His body was placed in the grave, His soul was put to grief in Sheol,[33] the realm of death, a place of torment[34] where for three days and three nights He paid the full wages of our sin.[35] When Death had exhausted its fury on Him for the guilt of our sins, it was no longer possible for Him to be held by its power.[36] That is when His soul and spirit returned to His body, which was waiting without decay in the grave,[37] and He rose triumphant over Death.

The Witness of the Resurrection

So after the untold millions of gallons of innocent blood shed by sacrificial animals, and after the Father's heart-wrenching sacrifice of His beloved Son, and after the Son's unimaginable suffering in death on our behalf, what should be the outcome? Will Yahshua see the fruit of the anguish of His soul in death and be satisfied?[38] What is the credible witness of His resurrection? Where are those whose life of love and unity is a living testimony to the end of death's reign? They could be found in the first century:

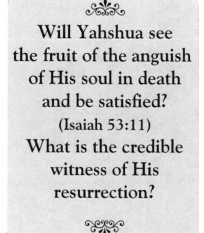

Will Yahshua see the fruit of the anguish of His soul in death and be satisfied? (Isaiah 53:11) What is the credible witness of His resurrection?

All of the believers were united, heart and soul; no one claimed private ownership of any possessions, as everything they owned was held in common. And with great power they gave witness to the resurrection of the Lord Jesus, and abundant grace was upon them all. (Acts 4:32-33)

They can also be found today, not among the 39,000 denominations of Christianity, but at the addresses listed in the back of this book, where all have truly laid their hands on the Lamb of God and obtained the forgiveness of their sins. The love of Messiah controls them, because they have concluded this: that One has died for all, therefore all have died; and He died for all, that those who live might no longer live for themselves but for Him who died and rose again on their behalf.[39] This is eternal life, and it begins as soon as death's reign comes to an end.

---

[33] Isaiah 53:10 [34] Luke 16:28 [35] Matthew 12:40 [36] Acts 2:24 [37] Acts 2:27,31
[38] Isaiah 53:11 [39] 2 Corinthians 5:14-15

SALVATION IS A FREE GIFT, BUT WHO IS IT GIVEN TO?

Salvation is freely given to those who
freely embrace the "hard words" of the gospel,
not explaining them away,
but gladly meeting the terms of peace.
Yahshua requires unconditional surrender
from those who would follow Him,
and immersion into the full-time life of a disciple.

The articles in this section
make the terms of peace very clear,
and refute the so-called gospel of cheap grace
marketed by the hucksters
of Christianity today.

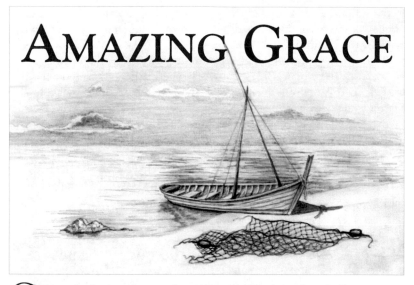

AMAZING GRACE

Grace... faith... works... such common words, but what do they mean? What is grace, and how does it work? What is faith, and where does it come from? Where does it lead? What are the works that cannot save us, and the works we are saved to do? For that matter, what is salvation, anyway? In his letter to the Ephesians, the apostle Paul was not preaching the gospel, but rather giving the disciples understanding about what had happened to them and what lay ahead of them — the process and the purpose of salvation. The *gospel* is found in the *Gospels*. The letters of Paul and the other apostles consist of instruction and correction for those who are already in salvation.[1] That is why we must look to the Gospels to find the foundation of these familiar terms Paul uses in his letters.

There is a process or a progression involved in salvation, and in the Gospels and the book of Acts there are many examples of people going through that process, or in some cases stopping short of salvation.

Grace

First comes *grace*, the unmerited favor of God. As it relates to salvation, grace is the working of God in a person's life to protect him, prepare him, and bring him to the right time and place to hear the gospel from someone who has been sent with the authority to proclaim it.[2]

It was *grace* to Peter that he had fished all night without catching anything, and that he happened to be cleaning his nets in that particular place where the Master wanted to teach that day, and that the Master chose his boat to speak from.[3] It was grace that caused the Master to pass

---

[1] It is ironic that most of the popular "plans of salvation" make little use of the Gospels and much improper use of Paul's letters. As a result, very few people have actually heard and obeyed the gospel.   [2] John 7:17-18   [3] Luke 5:1-10

by the sycamore tree where Zacchaeus was waiting, and to notice and call to him.[4] It was grace that caused the Ethiopian eunuch to happen to be passing near Philip and to be reading the scroll of the prophet Isaiah, and it was grace that caused Philip to hear from the Spirit the urging to approach the chariot and ask the eunuch whether he understood what he was reading.[5] And it was even grace to the "rich young ruler" that the Master came to teach in his town.[6]

So grace brings a person near in order to hear the good news. What happens next depends on the one who speaks and the one who hears.

Faith

Faith is *persuasion*. That is true both in the natural and the spiritual realm. A natural man can be persuaded in his mind to do many things, and it is a sort of faith, but the faith that saves is the persuasion of the Holy Spirit which comes to a person as he hears the gospel. As Paul said, "Faith comes by hearing, and hearing by the word of God."[7] But as Paul also labored to explain, the word of God must be spoken by a flesh-and-blood person who is "sent"[8] — that is, someone who has the spiritual authority to proclaim the gospel. The only thing that gives a person that spiritual authority is that he has obeyed the gospel himself and is living the life that it demands.[9]

So grace draws a person near to hear, and then through hearing the gospel from a true disciple, faith comes — but not automatically. It requires something very important, and very rare, on the part of the hearer: he must be willing to do the Father's will.[10] He must have ears to hear, which means a heart to obey.[11] Otherwise he will not submit to the spiritual authority of the one speaking; he will not receive him as coming from God.[12] He will not be persuaded, for he is in the grip of a stronger persuasion — the fear of losing his own life.[13]

> **Grace brings a person near to hear the good news, but what happens next depends on the one who speaks *and* the one who hears.**

[4] Luke 19:2-10   [5] Acts 8:27-39   [6] Mark 10:17-30   [7] Romans 10:17   [8] Romans 10:14-15; Matthew 10:40; John 13:20. There is not a single example in the New Testament of a person receiving the Holy Spirit without receiving a flesh-and-blood disciple filled with the Holy Spirit. So it is very odd that most Christians believe a person can become a disciple by simply reading a tract and saying a prayer, all by himself.   [9] John 7:18b; Otherwise he is living a lie and can only pass on the same deceitful spirit he is in fellowship with, according to John 7:18a; 2 Corinthians 4:2; 1 John 2:4; 2 Corinthians 11:13-15.   [10] John 7:17   [11] Matthew 13:9,15; Luke 14:26-35   [12] Matthew 10:40; John 13:20   [13] Hebrews 2:15; Luke 9:24; John 12:25; Revelation 21:7-8

That is what happened in the case of the "rich young ruler" who came asking what he must do to inherit eternal life:

> Then Jesus, looking at him, loved him, and said to him, "One thing you lack: Go your way, sell whatever you have and give to the poor, and you will have treasure in heaven; and come, take up the cross, and follow Me." But he was sad at this word, and went away sorrowful, for he had great possessions. (Mark 10:21-22)

Although there was abundant grace at work, bringing him into the very presence of the Master, he did not receive faith from hearing the gospel, but rather dread and gloom, for he was not willing to give up his own life, in order to receive the eternal life that Yahshua offered him. He loved his life in this world.

But in the case of the 3,000 on the day of Pentecost, we see a very different story. The *many other words*[14] they heard that day from Peter evidently imparted faith to them, for it says they "*gladly received* his word."[15] Gloom did not descend on them at the thought of giving up their lives, for they were fully persuaded that this Messiah was worth dying for. Thus they were baptized into His death and received the same Spirit that had filled the ones who spoke the good news to them.[16]

Belief that Impels Obedience

The *faith* that came to those 3,000 caused them to *believe* in their hearts in this Messiah whom they had crucified,[17] that He had paid for their sins through His death, and that He had risen from the dead and ascended to the right hand of the Father. And what happened next? Did they all go their separate ways, having added a new dimension to their lives? No. The message they heard called them to be saved from the perverse generation they were living in.[18] The Bible doesn't record the "many other words" Peter spoke to them that day, but we do know what the Master had commanded the apostles to do in the preaching of the gospel, which surely they were careful to obey:

> Therefore go and make disciples of all nations, baptizing them in the name of the Father and of the Son and of the Holy Spirit, and teaching them to obey everything I have commanded you. (Matthew 28:19-20)

So what was the first thing the Master had commanded them when He called them to follow Him? To forsake everything.[19] And lest we think that requirement applied only to the apostles, remember that after the woman broke her alabaster jar, her most precious possession, and poured out every drop of the fragrant oil upon Him, He instructed His disciples:

---

[14] Acts 2:40 [15] Acts 2:41 [16] Acts 2:38 (NKJV); Rom 6:2-5 [17] Acts 2:36
[18] Acts 2:40 [19] Mark 10:28; Luke 5:1-11; 14:33

I tell you the truth, wherever this gospel is preached throughout the world, what she has done will also be told, in memory of her. (Matthew 26:13)

It is doubtful that Peter would have forgotten to include this story in his *many other words*, considering how deeply it had affected the disciples the day it happened.[20] But regardless of the exact words Peter may have spoken, the outcome speaks for itself:

All the believers were together and had all things in common. Selling their possessions and goods, they gave to anyone as he had need. Every day they continued to meet together in the temple courts. They broke bread in their homes and ate together with glad and sincere hearts, praising God and enjoying the favor of all the people. And the Lord added to their number daily those who were being saved. (Acts 2:44-47)

It was neither a coincidence nor a misunderstanding that those 3,000 new disciples all gave up everything, including their independent lives, and shared a common life together.[21] Their belief *impelled*[22] obedience to what they heard. It was not merely a mental assent to the fact of Yahshua's death and resurrection. It was a total identification with Him and His people that cut them off from all past loyalties and occupations.

There is a belief that doesn't impel obedience. The Master encountered this kind of belief on several occasions, such as:[23]

Now while he was in Jerusalem at the Passover Feast, many people saw the miraculous signs he did and believed in his name. But Jesus would not entrust himself to them, for he knew all men. He did not need man's testimony about man, for he knew what was in a man. (John 2:23-25)

The words *believed* and *entrust* in this passage are actually the same word in the Greek manuscript. You could well say that they believed in Him but He didn't believe in them, for He knew it was only a belief in their minds and not in their hearts. They admired Him, but He knew they would not obey Him at all costs, therefore He could not entrust His Holy Spirit to them.[24]

So the faith that saves produces a belief that obeys; otherwise it is not saving faith. That is exactly what the writer of James was laboring to say:

Even so faith, if it has no works, is dead, being by itself. But someone may say, "You have faith and I have works; show me your faith without the works, and I will show you my faith by my works." You believe God is one? You do well; the demons also believe, and shudder. But are you willing to recognize, you foolish fellow, that faith without works is useless?
(James 2:17-20)

---

[20] Matthew 26:8,14-16   [21] Acts 4:32-35; 5:20   [22] *Impel* means to urge, constrain, or motivate a person to an action; to cause to move forward with force.   [23] John 8:30-44 is another vivid example of vain belief.   [24] Acts 5:32; Hebrews 5:9

Sadly, many are so foolish as to be unwilling to recognize the futility of a faith that does not result in the works that followed the first preaching of the gospel in Acts 2:42-47 and 4:32-37. But the Master said that those who have ears to hear will bear abundant fruit — thirty, sixty, or a hundredfold — and so prove to be His disciples.[25]

Works

Certainly, there are no works that a person can do to earn his salvation in Messiah. All of his good deeds have no more value than filthy rags in the currency of redemption.[26] It is only Messiah's worth that counts — the infinite value of His blood which He shed on our behalf.

In fact, anyone who really understands the futility of his own unredeemed life, with all the material manifestations of his own selfish works,[27] will be eager to abandon it all as soon as he discovers the pearl of great price.[28] It would not even enter the mind of someone who truly hates his own life in this world[29] that giving up his possessions in order to gain eternal life[30] could be considered "works salvation." He would be like Paul, who wrote,

> Yet indeed I also count all things loss for the surpassing value of knowing Christ Jesus my Lord, for whom I have suffered the loss of all things, and count them as rubbish,[31] in order that I may gain Christ. (Philippians 3:8)

Paul understood in the very core of his being what he was saved from and what he was saved *for*. The "loss of all things" was part of the practical reality of his old life being buried with Messiah in baptism,[32] not a "good work" that he did to earn his salvation.[33] Paul was glad to be free of his old life, career, and possessions so that he could lay hold of that for which Messiah had laid hold of him.[34] That is the revelation he had that caused him to write to the Ephesians,

> We are His workmanship, created in Christ Jesus for good works, which God prepared beforehand that we should walk in them. (Ephesians 2:10)

The word translated as *works* here (and in verse 9, for that matter) actually means *employment* or *occupation*. It is not speaking of isolated good deeds that one does from time to time, but rather the direction of one's will — what he does with his time, energy, skills, and strength. Everyone who is saved is saved for the purpose of spending the rest of his life employing his gifts[35] to build up the Body of Messiah:

---

[25] Matthew 13:3-9; John 15:8; 13:34-35; 1 John 3:14-18 [26] Isaiah 64:6 [27] Even if those past works looked good to the natural man, as in Titus 3:5. [28] Matthew 13:44-46 [29] John 12:25 [30] Mark 10:28-30; Luke 14:33 [31] The Greek word Paul used here means something worthless and detestable, such as the excrement of animals. [32] Romans 6:4-7 [33] Titus 3:5 [34] Philippians 3:12 [35] His "calling" or employment in the Body of Messiah, Ephesians 4:1.

From whom the whole body, joined and knit together by that which every joint supplies, according to the effective working by which every part does its share, causes growth of the body for the edifying of itself in love. This I say, therefore, and testify in the Lord, that you should no longer walk as the Gentiles walk, in the futility of their minds. (Ephesians 4:16-17)

Paul and the other apostles did not conceive of the Body of Messiah as a mystical union of isolated believers who live their own independent lives all week ("walk as the Gentiles walk"), and get together for an hour or two on Sunday. It was to be a full-time, visible demonstration of disciples living together in unity,[36] loving one another just as their Master had loved His first disciples[37] — 24 hours a day, 7 days a week — serving one another according to their gifts and abilities. Such people do not need to be concerned about what they will eat or what they will wear,[38] but can actually seek first His kingdom and His righteousness, knowing that all their needs will be met through the "effective working of every part" for the benefit of the whole. Such is the miracle of self-sacrificing love:[39]

If you love Me, keep My commandments. (John 14:15)

He who has My commandments and keeps them, it is he who loves Me. (John 14:21)

He who says, "I know Him," and does not keep His commandments, is a liar, and the truth is not in him. But whoever keeps His word, truly the love of God is perfected in him. By this we know that we are in Him. (1 John 2:4-5)

It is impossible to obey His commandments on your own. *It takes a community.* That is where the love of God is perfected in us — where we can truly love one another. That is where God has commanded the blessing of eternal life.[40]

Amazing Grace

The amazing thing about *grace* is that it brings about the purpose of God on the earth through willing human beings who receive *faith* when they hear the word of God, which causes them to *believe* to the point that they actually *obey* His commandments.[41] Together they bear the fruit of the Kingdom[42] — the life that bears witness to the fact that the Father actually sent His Son,[43] because "as He is, so also are they in this world."[44] ❧

---

[36] John 17:20-23   [37] John 13:34-35; 15:12-14   [38] Matthew 6:31-33
[39] 2 Corinthians 5:14-15   [40] Psalm 133:1-3   [41] John 14:15,21; Revelation 22:14 (KJV, NKJV)   [42] Matthew 21:43   [43] John 17:23   [44] 1 John 4:17

SAVED!
DAVE ✓
the Thief

say the
SINNERS
PRAYER
&
get
saved!

THE "SINNER'S PRAYER" VERSUS ROMANS 10:17

(Does Faith Come by Reading or Hearing?)

It has become an unquestioned assumption of Evangelical Christianity that a person can be saved merely by reading a tract and sincerely reciting the "Sinner's Prayer" printed on the back. After all, that's why this prayer is printed on the back of virtually every tract — so the reader can respond to what he reads by asking Jesus into his heart, whereupon he is assured that his sins are forgiven and he will go to heaven when he dies. More than likely, this new "born-again" believer is then advised to find himself a "Bible-believing church" where he can go on Sunday and be taught how to think as a Christian.

Ironically, if he actually succeeded in finding a *truly* Bible-believing church, he would soon discover that according to the Bible he was *not saved*. For as the Apostle Paul labored to explain, the faith that saves comes by *hearing* (not by *reading*) the gospel from someone who is sent with the grace and authority to proclaim it:

> For *"whoever calls on the name of the LORD shall be saved."*
> *How then shall they call on Him in whom they have not believed?*
> *And how shall they believe in Him of whom they have not heard?*
> *And how shall they hear without a preacher?*
> *And how shall they preach unless they are sent?*
> *As it is written: "How beautiful are the feet of those*
> *who preach the gospel of peace, who bring glad tidings of good things!"*
> *But they have not all obeyed the gospel. For Isaiah says,*
> *"Lord, who has believed our report?"*
> *So then, faith comes by hearing, and hearing by the word of God.*
> (Romans 10:13-17)

The progression is clear: In order to be *saved*, one has to *call* on the name of the Lord, and in order to *call* on Him with this effect, one has to *believe*, and in order to *believe*, one has to *hear* the "gospel of peace" from a *preacher*, and in order to *preach* so as to impart *faith* to the hearer, that *preacher* has to be *sent* with "beautiful feet" so as to have authority to command *obedience* to the gospel. It takes *all* of these ingredients in order for *saving faith* to be communicated to the heart of the hearer.

Jesus Himself put these ingredients in a nutshell when He spoke to some religious Jews who questioned His authority to teach:

> *"If anyone is willing to do His will, he will know of the teaching, whether it is of God or whether I speak from Myself. He who speaks from himself seeks his own glory; but He who is seeking the glory of the One who sent Him, He is true, and there is no unrighteousness in Him."* (John 7:17-18)

The hearer has to truly be willing to do the will of God, or he will not recognize the truth when he hears it. Also, the preacher must be without any deceit or falsehood or concern for his own fame or fortune,[1] but concerned only with rightly representing the One who sent him so as to pass on His Spirit to the willing hearer.

Coming to faith is not merely a matter of receiving *information*. If that were the case, then reading would be a sufficient mechanism to acquire saving faith. But faith is the persuasion of a *spirit* which is given voice by a human being who possesses that spirit. This is a spiritual principle which is true of any kind of faith, but in the case of *saving faith*, the spirit that persuades is the *Holy Spirit* speaking through a true believer who both possesses and is in fellowship with that Spirit.

---

[1] See also 2 Corinthians 4:2-5

That is why Jesus told His disciples, "He who receives you receives Me, and he who receives Me receives Him who sent Me."[2] He was sending them with the authority to act on His and His Father's behalf, in the power of the Spirit that was upon them through their fellowship with Him. And later, after His resurrection, they received the Holy Spirit in

> ❧
>
> **Ironically,
> if someone actually
> succeeded in finding
> a truly Bible-believing church,
> he would soon discover that
> according to the Bible,
> he is not saved.**
>
> ❧

their inner man (not just upon them), and He gave them authority not only to heal people but to impart the forgiveness He had purchased with His own blood.[3] It was with *that* authority that they preached on the Day of Pentecost, offering forgiveness and the Holy Spirit to all who would repent and be baptized.[4]

With *many other words*[5] Peter kept on exhorting them to "be saved from that perverse generation" which had killed their long-awaited Messiah. Those who had received his words were baptized. We can read what happened in Acts 2:42-47 and 4:32-37. We do not know exactly Peter's "many other words" — all we can see is the *result* that took place in the lives of those who heard his words.

The people were cut to the heart for crucifying the Messiah and cried out, "What shall we do?" So Peter obviously answered their question:

1) Having been cut to the heart, they must repent;

2) As a result of repenting they were to be baptized, calling on the name of Yahshua,[6] the Messiah;

3) As a result of being baptized, they would be forgiven for their sins;

4) As a result of being forgiven, they would be given the gift of the Holy Spirit;

5) As a result of receiving the Holy Spirit, they would continually devote themselves to the apostles' teaching;[7]

6) As a result of the apostles' teaching, "all who believed were together and had all things in common;"[8]

7) As a result of having all things in common, "they began selling

---

[2] Matthew 10:40; John 13:20; Luke 10:16   [3] John 14:17; 20:22   [4] Acts 2:38,41
[5] Acts 2:40   [6] *Yahshua* is the Hebrew name of the Savior; see *The Name Above All Names*, page 151.   [7] Acts 2:42   [8] Acts 2:44

their property and possessions and were equally sharing them with all, as anyone might have need."[9]

Peter told them that in the water they would be buried with their entire former life and all its ties and involvements. They would be plunged deep into Messiah, the Crucified One. The water was like His blood, and in this death they would be cutting themselves off from all demonic powers ruling this present age, demonstrating the victory of the Cross over them, and the removal of blood guilt from their heads.[10] In coming out of the water they would be the possessors of a new life in Messiah, having received the Holy Spirit to empower them to live in the victory and strength of the Risen One.

All who believed were together...

None who believed were alone.

They made a complete break with all and everything that would keep them from wholly devoting their lives to their brothers and sisters — the Body of Messiah of which they were now a part, having become "bone of their bone and flesh of their flesh."[11] From then on they were committed to live and to die for the cause they had embraced — a consecration unto death. In obedience to their confession made in baptism they came into such grave conflicts with their relatives (i.e., those who would not obey the gospel) that households were dissolving, families were split, engagements were canceled, and marriages were torn apart.[12] They were hated by the world, especially the religious establishment, just as their Master Yahshua had promised.[13]

Of course, the 3000 who were saved that day submitted their very lives and possessions to those who had preached the gospel to them, and the apostles took care of them, seeing to it that everyone's needs were met.[14] Being "born again" wasn't just a religious experience — it was the practical reality of their lives, for they were born as spiritual babes into a new family, never to return to the perverse society from which they had been delivered. They didn't have to go "find a Bible-believing church," for they were immediately immersed into a full-time life of devotion to Messiah *in His Body.* "All who believed were together and had all things in common."[15] *None who believed were alone,* living their own independent lives in the world and just going to church on Sunday.

Whoever has the Son has the Life. To have the Son, you must receive those whom He sends who already have His life.[16] This is

---

[9] Acts 2:45   [10] Matthew 27:25   [11] Mark 3:33-35   [12] Matthew 10:34-39; Luke 12:49-53; 14:26; Mark 10:28-30   [13] John 15:18-21; 16:2   [14] Acts 2:42-47; 4:32-37   [15] Acts 2:44   [16] John 13:20

surrender into the arms of His Body, becoming totally vulnerable, which is the sustenance of eternal life. This is what it means to be "in Him." There is no one saved apart from total vulnerability to all He is and says, without fear or doubt. It requires no less surrender than Luke 14:31-32, proven by verse 33.

> [31] "Or what king, going to make war against another king, does not sit down first and consider whether he is able with ten thousand to meet him who comes against him with twenty thousand? [32] Or else, while the other is still a great way off, he sends a delegation and asks conditions of peace. [33] So likewise, whoever of you does not forsake all that he has cannot be My disciple."

You can't receive the King by just saying the "Sinner's Prayer." To receive the King, you have to receive the delegation He sends. You have to consider their feet "beautiful" who bring the terms of peace,[17] laying everything at their feet.[18] If you receive the sent one, you receive the King; if you receive Him, you receive His Father.[19] If you reject the sent one, you reject the Son and the Father.[20]

Yahshua is the Mediator between God and man, but Yahshua's disciples are the mediators or ambassadors[21] who bring men to Messiah. If the thought that no one can be saved by the "faith" they receive through reading a tract or even the Bible upsets you, it *should*! Countless people have been bamboozled into thinking they are saved and going to heaven as a result of saying the "Sinner's Prayer" all by themselves, or even as a result of hearing the preaching of someone who does not himself have the Holy Spirit or the true gospel, but is seeking his own glory.[22]

The simple fact is this: there is not a *single example* in the whole New Testament of a person being saved apart from receiving a true, flesh-and-blood disciple with the true gospel on his lips.[23] That true disciple will bring the newly born-again believer into a true full-time life where he no longer lives by or for himself,[24] but is fully devoted to the One who died and rose again on his behalf.[25] So where is that full-time life of devotion to Messiah?

You can find it at all the Bible-believing communities listed in the back of this book, where you are welcome to come and hear the Good News and see it being lived out day by day. ✤

---

[17] Romans 10:15 [18] Acts 4:34-35 [19] Matthew 10:40 [20] Luke 10:16
[21] 2 Corinthians 5:19-20 [22] 2 Corinthians 2:17 [23] Even Paul had to receive the one sent to him in order to be saved in baptism (Acts 22:6-16). [24] Acts 2:44
[25] 2 Corinthians 5:14-15

the BARRIER

He has delivered us from the domain of darkness and transferred us into the kingdom of His beloved Son, in whom we have redemption, the forgiveness of sins. (Colossians 1:13-14)

For nearly three decades a great wall of concrete and razor wire divided East and West Berlin, a quite visible boundary between two opposing domains. West Berlin was a small island of relative freedom in the midst of a vast empire of tyranny. Millions of oppressed souls longed for the freedom of the West, but for most it was only an impossible dream. Still, a few courageous ones overcame almost insurmountable obstacles and escaped through tunnels under the wall, through which they had to crawl on their hands and knees. They could take nothing with them — only the clothes on their backs — but they were happy to leave everything behind for the hope of starting a new life.

Although only temporal, the example of the Berlin Wall can help us to "see" the unseen but very real barrier that separates the domain of darkness from the kingdom of light, and understand what it takes to get from one to the other.

The Domain of Darkness

The whole world lies in the power of the evil one.[1] All men are born under his sway.[2] Although all men have a free will, and a conscience by which they know good from evil,[3] they are alienated from God due to their sin and must strive to make their own way in this world.[4] Their ingrained insecurity and self-interest make them easy prey for the evil prince of this world, whose chief occupation is to lead them astray.[5] Were it not for the conscience, human society would probably have ended long ago, but now the restraint of conscience has given way to the insatiable demands of self to the point that the very foundations of morality have all but crumbled.[6]

---

[1] 1 John 5:19 [2] Ephesians 2:2 [3] Genesis 3:22 [4] Genesis 3:17-19
[5] Revelation 12:9 [6] Psalm 12:1

Such is the nature of this world. It runs on the engine of self-interest. The souls of men — their intellect, will, and emotions — are consumed with their own needs and desires, with advancing their own careers, causes, and reputations, and with maintaining and building up the systems of this world order.[7] Their conflicting desires and ambitions are the cause of immeasurable human misery and the looming destruction of the very planet they grudgingly share. Their eyes cannot see any way out of the cycle of sin and death they are trapped in. Even their religion does not set them free, but only comforts them in their prison. They sit in darkness and in the shadow of death.[8]

The Kingdom of Light

Onto the battered landscape of human history walked an ordinary-looking Man with an extraordinary message:

> *The Spirit of the Lord is upon me, because he has anointed me to preach good news to the poor. He has sent me to proclaim release to the captives and recovery of sight to the blind, to set at liberty those who are oppressed, to proclaim the acceptable year of the Lord. (Luke 4:18-19)*

From the day that He severed Himself in baptism from the fallen religious system of His day,[9] He spoke of nothing but the *gospel of the kingdom*.[10] He filled His disciples and all who would listen with the vision of a new social order based on love — the direct opposite of the self-interest that fuels the domain of darkness. For by *love* He did not mean merely an emotion, but rather the deliberate activation of one's will to seek the welfare of another without regard for one's own benefit or loss.[11] He did not envision occasional heroic deeds of love adorning the typical routines of life in this world. He lived and died to bring about a whole society of people who take no thought for themselves,[12] but spend their

---

[7] 1 John 2:16   [8] Luke 1:79   [9] Matthew 3:1-15   [10] References in the Gospels for "gospel of the kingdom" and "kingdom of heaven" and "kingdom of God" are too numerous to cite, which makes it all the more striking that today's fallen religious system avoids the topic entirely.   [11] Luke 9:23-24   [12] Matthew 6:31-33

lives each and every day serving one another. That is what He meant by seeking first the kingdom of God.

The Master had absolutely no expectation of this new social order filling the earth in this age. He did not commission His disciples to make the world a better place by infiltrating the world's society, industry, or government.[13] On the contrary, He called them to come out of that fallen system,[14] even at the cost of their family ties,[15] in order to follow Him. Together they would form a "city" set on a hill; together they would be a light to the world around them.[16] Their *cities* (communities) would be islands of refuge in the midst of a world in bondage to the evil one[17] — a foretaste of the fullness of Messiah's kingdom that will fill the whole earth in the next age when the evil one is bound.[18]

However, that foretaste of the coming kingdom could not come about until the Messiah had died as a ransom for all[19] and risen from the dead and ascended to His Father in heaven. Then His Spirit could be released to fill the waiting disciples and empower them to do everything the Master had taught them about the kingdom of God.[20] It is no accident that the very first thing that happened when the Holy Spirit was poured out upon them was that they spoke the gospel of the kingdom with boldness, and three thousand men responded to the call to "be saved from this perverse generation" by utterly forsaking their old lives to live a common life together.[21] It was the normal and only fitting response to the good news of the One who had died to ransom them from the clutches of the evil one and his dark domain. Their common life of love and unity was the witness of the kingdom[22] — the evidence that He was actually ruling in their midst.[23]

The Barrier between the Kingdoms

Although the book of Acts tells this story in only a few sentences, each of those 3000 men had to overcome his own personal obstacles to surrendering his life. There were many wives and children, parents and siblings, farms and businesses, employees, possessions, and debts to be considered. Probably not all of their families and friends were overjoyed at the decisions they made that day to give up everything to follow this resurrected Messiah who could only be seen in His people. It took great courage for those men to walk out the confessions of faith they made that day, at any cost.[24]

---

[13] 2 Timothy 2:4 [14] John 15:19; 2 Corinthians 6:14-18 [15] Matthew 10:34-39; Mark 10:29-30 [16] Matthew 5:14-16 — The Master was addressing His disciples collectively, not as independent individuals. The word "you" in Matthew 5:14 is plural, while the words "light" and "city" are singular. [17] Philippians 2:15 [18] Revelation 20:1-3 [19] 1 Timothy 2:6 [20] Matthew 28:19-20; Acts 1:3; John 14:26; 7:37-39 [21] Acts 2:40-47 [22] Matthew 24:14 [23] Even today, where He is truly being made Lord, the same common life will prove it. [24] Matthew 10:34-39

The barrier that holds men captive in the domain of darkness, although invisible, is every bit as real as was the Berlin Wall. Instead of concrete and wire, it is woven of fear, shame, insecurity, intimidation, anxiety, peer pressure, emotional attachments, pride, and countless worldly entanglements. When someone is truly weary of his servitude to the evil prince of this world and the weight of his own guilt, and hears the voice of the Righteous One through His servants, and is drawn to the light emanating from their camp, he or she will inevitably come face-to-face with this barrier. All manner of obstacles will bar the way — an unwilling spouse, rebellious children, financial responsibilities, the pleas, promises, threats, and warnings of family and friends... The tentacles of the unseen realm of darkness will reach out through every earthly tie to tighten their grip on any who dare attempt escape.

It is not that the blood of Yahshua was insufficient to pay the ransom for all, but all are not willing to do His will.[25] All are not thirsty enough to overcome every obstacle that keeps them from drinking the water of life:

> I will give of the fountain of the water of life freely to him who thirsts. He who overcomes shall inherit all things, and I will be his God and he shall be My son. But the cowardly and unbelieving and abominable and murderers and sexually immoral and sorcerers and idolaters and all liars shall have their part in the lake that burns with fire and sulfur, which is the second death. (Revelation 21:6-8)

Those who are too cowardly to overcome the obstacles betray the fact of their unbelief. Preferring the pitiful comforts of their captivity,[26] they show contempt for the blood that was shed for them and become guilty of it, classing themselves as the worst of criminals.[27]

There is no toll gate at the entrance to the kingdom of light. The abundant life of the Son of God is freely given. But just like that tunnel under the Berlin Wall, the way of escape that leads to the kingdom is narrow and difficult, and few are they who even find it.[28] Nothing of the old life can pass through it, which is why only those who hate their life in this world will be able to make the passage.[29] They are the only ones who will be united with Him in the likeness of His death, and serve Him where He is. ✣

> For if we have been united together in the likeness of His death, certainly we also shall be in the likeness of His resurrection, knowing this, that our old man was crucified with Him, that the body of sin might be done away with, that we should no longer be slaves of sin. For he who has died has been freed from sin. (Romans 6:5-7)

---

[25] John 7:17; Hebrews 5:9; Acts 5:32 [26] Luke 6:24 [27] Matthew 11:23-24
[28] Matthew 7:13-14 [29] John 12:25-26

THIRSTING FOR THE WATER OF LIFE

He will give the water of life (the Holy Spirit) freely
to anyone who is thirsty enough to overcome every obstacle
that stands in the way of obeying the gospel.

You've probably lived all your life in towns and never been in a desert, but there is a vivid image imprinted in your mind of a man crawling across the sand towards water. He is thirsty, dying of thirst, but the cool oasis is a mirage; the water he sees does not exist. The costly waste of precious effort — only one who was truly thirsty would risk it all again at another promise of water. Would this oasis be real or another bitter disappointment?

The Woman at the Well[1]

So many times she had been to the well to draw water. It was part of life. Every gallon used for cooking and washing had to be fetched in heavy clay jars. So many times a day, she, like everyone else, came to get water. So much water was needed for their animals and for themselves, for their daily existence, and yet the well had never run dry. The people had been drinking from it for many generations. Deep beneath the dry ground the water had a source that had not failed them. Without it, they could not live, and she knew better than we how precious a source of water is.

When the man at the well offered her "living water" she could only wonder where He could get better water than was in the well. She had not yet perceived that He was speaking of the spiritual realm. Then He said that the water He gave would become a spring of water that would well up in her to eternal life. Oh, what water was this? She desired more than the humdrum life of drawing water and just living. She asked Him for this water that held the promise of life. But was she willing to pay the price?

"Go, call your husband, and come back."

"I have no husband."

"You are right in saying, 'I have no husband,' for you have had five husbands, and the one you have now is not your husband. What you have said is true."

[1] John 4:5-43

Ohhh! That hurt! How did He know that? It seemed like He could look right into her soul. Five marriages… five disappointments… All her life she had thirsted for a covenant relationship that would fulfill something deep in her soul, but it always eluded her. She went into each marriage with such hope that it would satisfy her, but each time hope evaporated like a mirage. Finally she had given up hope, not daring to open up her heart to another man, but just settling for mere physical pleasure as long as it lasted. But it troubled her conscience, and this man saw right through her outward composure. She struggled to overcome the urge to just run away. But obviously this man was a prophet, a man of God. Maybe He could answer some of her nagging questions…

"How is it that we worship according to the faith of our fathers, but you Jews say that God doesn't accept our worship or hear our prayers?"

That question had never come to rest in her. She had tried to fill up her soul with many things, but still she was empty. Nothing had satisfied her. She was still thirsty, and the offer of "living water" that would well up like a spring within her was very appealing, and she was willing to face the shame of her sin and the futility of her life in order to receive that living water.

The Bible does not say much more about this woman's life beyond the fact that she excitedly told everyone in her village that she had met the Messiah and how He had told her "everything she ever did." The effect this had on them was amazing, considering two undeniable facts: 1) Small villages being what they are, everyone knew very well what this woman's life was like, and what "everything she ever did" entailed; and 2) Most people would not want anyone to tell them everything they ever did. But evidently there were many thirsty people in that village, for they overcame the natural urge to keep the walls up around their hurting souls and they compelled the Master to stay there and teach them, and it says that many believed in Him.

Living Water

What is this "living water" that the Master offered to the woman at the well? Is it available to just anyone? How does one receive it? And how do you know that you have it? These are vital[2] questions. You may be surprised at some of the answers that are found in the Scriptures, which are not the traditional answers you may have heard in church.

---

[2] *Vital* means necessary to sustain life.

The first question is answered very clearly a few chapters later in the gospel according to John:

> On the last day, that great day of the feast, Jesus stood and cried out, saying, "If anyone thirsts, let him come to Me and drink. He who believes in Me, as the Scripture says, out of his heart will flow rivers of living water." But this He spoke concerning the Spirit, whom those believing in Him would receive; for the Holy Spirit was not yet given, because Jesus was not yet glorified. (John 7:37-39)

So "living water" is the Holy Spirit, right? That's not so surprising. You may have been told that you already have this living water, if ever you said the "sinner's prayer" and asked Jesus into your heart. After all, the Holy Spirit, like salvation, is a free gift, right?

The Holy Spirit is given freely, but who is He given to? To understand this, you must look more closely at the Master's words. He said, "If anyone thirsts, let him come to Me and drink." So you have to be thirsty, truly longing for spiritual life that you don't yet have (for the Master told the woman that whoever drinks of this water will never thirst again).

Coming to Him

And then you have to come to Him. Where is He? Now you may think this means you just need to "draw near to Him in your heart" or something like that, since, after all, He is literally in heaven right now so you can't physically go to Him, right? Wrong! Another time, the Master said:

> He who loves his life will lose it, and he who hates his life in this world will keep it for eternal life. If anyone serves Me, let him follow Me; and where I am, there My servant will be also… (John 12:25-26)

The first sentence describes someone who is thirsty, not satisfied with his life in this world. Then it says that someone like that who desires to serve Him must serve where He is. Where is He? He is where His Body is — where His disciples are living together in unity, in community. That's where eternal life is.[3] Now there is a lot written about this elsewhere in this book, which I will not go into here. But suffice it to say that nowhere in the New Testament is there a single example of a person getting saved or receiving the Holy Spirit apart from receiving a flesh-and-blood disciple (sent from a community of disciples) who preached the good news to him.[4] The notion that a person can pick up a tract on a park bench and say the "sinner's prayer" and ask Jesus into his heart, all by himself, is totally foreign to the Word of God.[5]

---

[3] Psalm 133:1-3   [4] Matthew 10:40; John 13:20   [5] See also *The Sinner's Prayer versus Romans 10:17* on page 109 for more about this fallacy.

What it Means to Drink

So in order to receive the water of life, you must be thirsty, and you must come to Him, and then you must drink. What then does it mean to drink? The thirsty man in the desert gives all his strength to get to the oasis he sees in the distance, but if it is only a mirage, his effort is wasted — he cannot drink. But what if it is real? What will he do then? With great joy he would immerse himself in that water and drink to his heart's content! He will live and not die. Can we relate this to the Master's words?

> *"If anyone thirsts, let him come to Me and drink. He who believes in Me, as the Scripture says, out of his heart will flow rivers of living water."* But *this He spoke concerning the Spirit, whom those believing in Him would receive…* (John 7:38-39)

Clearly, to drink is to believe in Him. So what does it mean to believe in Him? According to the latest statistics, approximately two billion people claim to believe in Him. Are there really two billion people on the earth who have rivers of living water flowing from their inmost being? That is about one third of the world population. But the Master said:

> *Enter by the narrow gate; for wide is the gate and broad is the way that leads to destruction, and there are many who go in by it. But narrow is the gate and difficult is the way which leads to life, and there are few who find it.* (Matthew 7:13-14)

Surely those two billion "believers" are not the few the Master spoke of. Even if you estimated that only half of them — one billion — were really serious about their Christian faith, could that be considered the few? Did you ever consider that what He meant by believing in Him might be fundamentally different from the popular understanding?

Believing in Him as the Scripture Says

Perhaps there is a hint here: "He who believes in Me as the Scripture says…" Most translations associate the phrase "as the Scripture says" with the words that follow it rather than the words that precede it, but remember, there was no punctuation in the original Greek manuscripts, so it is up to the translator to supply it according to the context. If the phrase "as the Scripture says" refers to what follows it, you would expect that to be a quotation or at least a paraphrase of something in the Old Testament scriptures, but there is nothing even close. We take it as prophetic of the Master's words and the apostles' writings being recorded and preserved as the New Testament scriptures. In that light, the Master was speaking of those who believe in Him according to what the Scriptures say it means to believe in Him.

You see, it is entirely possible to "believe in Him" apart from salvation. For example:

Now while he was in Jerusalem at the Passover Feast, many people saw the miraculous signs he was doing and believed in him. But Jesus would not entrust himself to them, for he knew all men. (John 2:23-24)

They believed in Him, but He did not believe in them![6] They believed, but not in the way the Scriptures say you must believe in order for Him to entrust Himself (give His Holy Spirit) to you. He only gives His Holy Spirit to those who obey Him.[7]

So how do the Scriptures say you must believe in Him in order to have rivers of living water flow from your inmost being? What does it mean to drink? The Master spoke about drinking another time, and what He said totally separated the true believers from those who only believed in their minds:

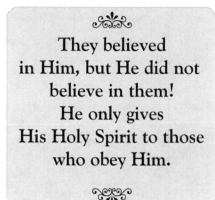

They believed in Him, but He did not believe in them! He only gives His Holy Spirit to those who obey Him.

Then Jesus said to them, "Most assuredly, I say to you, unless you eat the flesh of the Son of Man and drink His blood, you have no life in you. Whoever eats My flesh and drinks My blood has eternal life, and I will raise him up at the last day. For My flesh is food indeed, and My blood is drink indeed. He who eats My flesh and drinks My blood abides in Me, and I in him… From that time many of His disciples went back and walked with Him no more. Then Jesus said to the twelve, "Do you also want to leave?" But Simon Peter answered Him, "Lord, to whom shall we go? You have the words of eternal life. Also we have come to believe and know that You are the Christ, the Son of the living God." (John 6:53-69)

What was the difference between those who left and those who stayed? Those who stayed had nowhere else to go. Oh, it's not that they couldn't have gone back to their old jobs and families. Physically they could have done that. But in their hearts they were totally identified with their Master, totally devoted to Him and dependent upon Him as their source of life. They had all left everything to follow Him[8] — their possessions, their occupations, their causes, and even their families. They believed in Him with their whole hearts, entrusting their whole lives to

---

[6] The word translated *believe* in verse 23 is the same as the word translated *entrust* in verse 24.   [7] Acts 5:32   [8] Mark 10:28

Him, and even when He said things that shocked them, things they couldn't understand, they trusted Him.

Here some of the other shocking things He said:

> *If anyone comes to Me and does not hate his father and mother, wife and children, brothers and sisters, yes, and his own life also, he cannot be My disciple... So therefore, no one of you can be My disciple who does not give up all his own possessions. (Luke 14:26,33)*

> *Do not think that I came to bring peace on earth. I did not come to bring peace but a sword. For I have come to set a man against his father, a daughter against her mother, and a daughter-in-law against her mother-in-law; and a man's enemies will be those of his own household. He who loves father or mother more than Me is not worthy of Me. And he who loves son or daughter more than Me is not worthy of Me. And he who does not take his cross and follow after Me is not worthy of Me. He who finds his life will lose it, and he who loses his life for My sake will find it. (Matthew 10:34-39)*

You can water His words down all you like, but whoever does not drink them full strength is not really thirsty for eternal life, and will not receive the life the Master promised those who believe in Him enough to obey Him.

> **You can water His words down all you like, but whoever does not drink them full strength is not really thirsty for eternal life.**

He Who Overcomes

Notice that the Master spoke of those who were not worthy of Him. Most Christians are not used to thinking in terms of being "worthy" of belonging to or being identified with Christ because they have received a false understanding about the "free gift" of salvation and have revulsion toward anything that sounds like "works salvation." Indeed, salvation is a free gift, but who is it given to? Only those who show by their obedience to the gospel that Christ is worth more to them than their own life and possessions. It does require effort to obtain the gift of eternal life, as is clear from His words here:

> *And He said to me, "It is done! I am the Alpha and the Omega, the Beginning and the End. I will give of the fountain of the water of life freely to him who thirsts. He who overcomes shall inherit all this, and I will be his God and he shall be My son. (Revelation 21:6-7)*

He will give the water of life (the Holy Spirit) freely to anyone who is thirsty enough to overcome every obstacle that stands in the way of obeying the gospel. That is what it means to drink. The one who is truly thirsty will gladly[9] give up his possessions, his career, his social status — all that "his life in this world"[10] consists of — for the sake of the treasure he has found. He will overcome the opposition of family and friends who try to dissuade him from abandoning all for the gospel's sake. He will overcome the tugs of his own emotional attachments to the comforts, pleasures, and security of his old life, as well as the fears of being ridiculed and ostracized by his peers.

Indeed, there is much to overcome in order to obey the true gospel of the kingdom. And those who fail to overcome all that must be overcome in order to obey the gospel will also fail to inherit eternal life. Instead, they will inherit eternal death, for that is what the very next verse says:

> But the cowardly and unbelieving, the abominable, murderers, sexually immoral, sorcerers, idolaters, and all liars shall have their part in the lake which burns with fire and brimstone, which is the second death." (Revelation 21:8)

The attributes "cowardly and unbelieving" go together, in contrast to the courageous believers of the previous verse who overcame all opposition in order to drink the water of life. It is not speaking of those who never heard the true gospel and therefore had no opportunity to believe unto eternal life, but of those who did hear the gospel but were too cowardly to obey it. Such ones do not consider our Master worthy of surrendering their life and all they possess, and He does not consider them worthy of receiving His life. In rejecting the living water He freely offers, they make themselves worthy of leading the pack of abominable perverts, murderers, adulterers, sorcerers, idolaters, and liars who shall have their part in the lake of fire.

We sincerely hope that you are not one of them, but are instead truly thirsty for eternal life. Just as the Master offered the woman at the well, we offer to you the living water that has fully satisfied us.[11] But you have to drink it *freely*, that is, without a cause to hold you back. He will give the water of life freely to those who will drink it freely, without anything held in reserve. ※

> "And the Spirit and the bride say, 'Come!' And let him who hears say, 'Come!' And let him who thirsts come. Whoever desires, let him take the water of life freely." (Revelation 22:17)

---

[9] Matthew 13:44   [10] John 12:25   [11] John 4:13-14

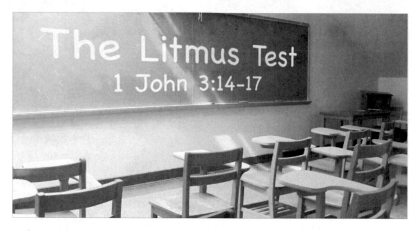

The Litmus Test
1 John 3:14-17

A "litmus test" is a test in which a single factor is decisive in proving the presence or absence of something. "I have eternal life," many will say, but passing the litmus test determines whether someone has truly believed *as the Scriptures say.*

> In the last day, that great day of the feast, Jesus stood and cried out, saying, "If anyone thirsts, let him come to Me and drink. He who believes in Me as the Scripture has said, out of his heart will flow rivers of living water." But this He spoke concerning the Spirit, whom those believing in Him would receive; for the Holy Spirit was not yet given, because Jesus was not yet glorified" (John 7:37-39)

> Jesus answered and said to her, "If you knew the gift of God, and who it is who says to you, 'Give Me a drink,' you would have asked Him, and He would have given you living water [the Holy Spirit]." ... whoever drinks of the water that I will give him shall never thirst; but the water that I will give him will become in him a well of water springing up to eternal life." (John 4:10,14)

So how do the scriptures say one must believe in order to have this river of living water flowing out of him? For the scriptures give us the litmus test in order that we could know whether we have passed from death to life and have truly received the Holy Spirit — the *Water of Life.* John 5:24 presents the good news in very clear and simple terms:

> Most assuredly, I say to you, he who hears My word and believes Him who sent Me has everlasting life, and shall not come into judgment, but has passed from death into life.

But how does anyone *know* he is saved? Does he know because the preacher tells him so? Is it enough to hear, "I know that I know that I know I am saved"? It wasn't enough for me. I still wasn't *sure.* Something very deep seemed to be missing. Then I discovered — well, friends showed me — the marvelous first letter of John. It tells everyone how they can *know*. It gives all of us the litmus test. Take it yourself. Read through First John, then especially consider chapter 3, verses 14, 16, and 17. They utterly disqualify mere mental belief:

> [14]*We know that we have passed from death to life, because we love the brethren. He who does not love his brother abides in death.* [16]*By this we know love, because He laid down His life for us. And we also ought to lay down our lives for the brethren.* [17]*But whoever has this world's goods, and sees his brother in need, and shuts up his heart from him, how does the love of God abide in him?*

The Test

The criterion for the litmus test is verse 14 — "Do you love the brethren?" When a person has been saved, and has passed from death into life, and partaken of the water of life, the inevitable result will be that he sacrificially loves his brothers. The presence or absence of true salvation will be revealed by the results of the litmus test.

"I love my brothers and sisters in the Lord," most would say, and that was my first response, I must admit. Most people would claim to love the brethren, so how could that be the litmus test for true salvation?

The answer: We must define our terms the way the Bible does, and the way the Apostle John did. He gives the definition for "love" in verse 16: "we *know* love, because He laid down His life for us. And we also ought to lay down our lives for the brethren." How did the Son of God demonstrate love? By laying down His life every day for His disciples and for others, not considering His own needs, sharing everything that He had, considering even the outcasts and the lowly, appealing to the high-minded and proud, even sacrificing His very life for the good of others. This is the love of God, and this is the factor that is poured into the heart of a person who is truly saved.[1]

Verse 17 defines the test results even further. If a person has something and he sees a brother in need, if he does not share what he has, it is proof-negative for the love of God being present in His heart. Selfishness, greed, accumulations of possessions, and lacks of sharing indicate that true salvation is not present.

We can see the proof-positive results of a people who passed the litmus test in Acts 2:42 — "All who believed shared all things in common… And there were no needy among them, for they shared everything in common." But later, when the letter of 1 John was written, the church was filled with many people who had a kind of belief, but it was not saving belief, as they were not able to demonstrate, try though they might, the proving factor of loving as the Son of God had loved.

---

[1] Romans 5:5

That's why 1 John was written; its sole purpose was that those who read it could know whether they had really received saving faith. For the Savior and the apostles knew that people could believe in vain[2] (as I had, and maybe you have), but their heart still reached out to them. John put something special in 1 John 5:13 — a provision, just for those who didn't pass the litmus tests of 1 John 2:4, 3:17, and 4:20.

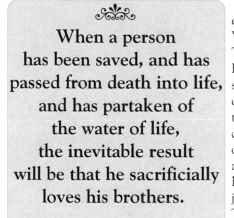

When a person has been saved, and has passed from death into life, and has partaken of the water of life, the inevitable result will be that he sacrificially loves his brothers.

Some would claim to see, even though they were blind, as Yahshua spoke of in John 9:41. Their guilt can't be removed. But those who *don't* claim to see, and so don't have the confidence after reading 1 John that they have passed out of death into life, still have an opportunity to believe and love as their Master commanded all His disciples to love, which was just as He had loved them.[3] The Authorized Version gets this very important verse right:

These things have I written unto you that believe on the name of the Son of God; that ye may know that ye have eternal life, and that ye may believe on the name of the Son of God. (1 John 5:13)

That is why John repeats the phrase "believe on the name of the Son of God" in verse 13. So 1 John 5:12-13 struck home to some in John's day who thought they had believed on the name of the Son, but discovered, after reading the letter, that they could not confess they had truly passed out of death and into life. In fact, they were now sure that the love of God did not abide in their hearts. After this rude awakening, they took hope in John's promise that they could yet believe and surrender their life to the True One whom John knew.[4]

In every other translation you can see how they tried to make sense out of this seemingly confusing verse. But understanding the intentions of John in writing this makes it clear that he wasn't being redundant in what he was saying. So you could read it: "These things have I written unto you that believe on the name of the Son of God; that ye may know that ye have eternal life, and that ye may [still have an opportunity to] believe on the name of the Son of God [if you can honestly see that your life doesn't match up to everything that is written in this letter]."

---

[2] John 2:23-25; 8:30-44; 1 Corinthians 15:2   [3] John 13:34-35   [4] 1 John 5:20

Confidence Towards God

The litmus test of 1 John reveals the presence or absence of the love of God. Paul wrote in Romans 5:5 that "the love of God has been poured out in our hearts by the Holy Spirit." The book of 1 John lets anyone know who wants to know whether this has actually happened in his life, or whether he only has the concept of love without the power to love.

> My little children, let us not love in word or in tongue, but in deed and in truth. And by this we know that we are of the truth, and shall assure our hearts before Him. For if our heart condemns us, God is greater than our heart, and knows all things. Beloved, if our heart does not condemn us, we have confidence toward God. (1 John 3:18-21)

In these verses, John is not teaching that even though our heart condemns us for failing to love our brother in deed and truth, God overlooks it and does not hold us guilty for not loving and not obeying His word. That is why the next verse says that if our hearts don't condemn us (because we do love our brothers), then we have confidence towards God. If we are not loving as He loved, then we do not and we cannot have confidence towards God. Indeed, He knows our heart. He knows in a greater and more comprehensive way than we do why and how we fail to love. And, He does not overlook it. He is not partial.

Those Who Have the Son Have the Life

Those who have the Son have the life,[5] which is the one thing I knew I didn't have, caught up as I was in the rat race, like everyone else. No matter how much I did, being part of the church council, Sunday School Superintendent, giving of my time and money, my daily life was much the same as everyone in the world around me. The only practical difference was that I went to church on Wednesday evening and on Sunday, and they didn't. The void inside of me and the lack of confidence that I was saved never went away.

The first believers seemed to have something I didn't have. They had not only received *the whole message of this new life*, as the angel told Peter to preach in Acts 5:20, but they had received *the life* itself. And it was a *life together*! That was the difference. Seeing that opened up the reality of what it meant to believe. To *believe* means to be persuaded in one's heart of the truth by the Holy Spirit through hearing the gospel from a righteous sent one, as the Savior spoke of in John 7:18. Such a one is true because he is not seeking his own glory, but the glory of the One who sent him. And such a one is spiritually and morally clean, for Yahshua said, "There is no unrighteousness in him."

---

[5] 1 John 5:12 in the NASB reads, "He who has the Son has the life; he who does not have the Son of God does not have the life."

How could anyone have truly believed in the True One without a true preacher speaking the very Word of Messiah?[6] The one who is doing the Father's will must meet the one who is willing to do the Father's will. The hearer is then given the needed illumination by the Father as our Master said, "He shall know of the teaching, whether it is of God."[7] The gospel is then the power of God for salvation, and the Father communicates the "good gift" of the Holy Spirit to those who are persuaded to die to themselves, take up their cross, and do His will.

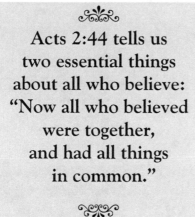

Acts 2:44 tells us two essential things about all who believe: "Now all who believed were together, and had all things in common."

John 3:16 is probably the best known and most loved verse in the Bible, "For God so loved the world that He gave His only begotten Son, that whoever believes in Him should not perish but have everlasting life." But what does it mean to *believe* as this verse says, to put one's complete trust in the Savior of the world?[8] The Scriptures tell all of us plainly, if we are willing to listen. The word *believes* in John 3:16 is the same Greek word as *believed* in Acts 2:44, which tells us two absolutely essential things about all who believe: *"Now all who believed were together, and had all things in common."*

This was very good news to me, because when I found the people who lived the life of faith, it meant I had also found a place to belong, a place to call home — true community.

Epistle of Straw?

Some in John's day obviously were not in fellowship with God, as 1 John 1:6 says. And they were not in fellowship with John either, which is why he writes his letter:

That which we have seen and heard we declare to you, that you also may have fellowship with us; and truly our fellowship is with the Father and with His Son Jesus Christ. (1 John 1:3)

John, of course, knew all about abiding in Him and bearing fruit, because the love of God was in his heart. He had borne much fruit and so had proven to be one of His disciples. That was all John wanted for those who believed in Yahshua through his message. John used the word

<hr />

[6] Romans 10:14-17   [7] John 7:17   [8] The word *believe* (*pisteuo*) is #4100 in Strong's Greek Concordance. It comes from #4102 (*pistis*), persuasion, which is derived from #3982 (*peitho*), meaning to convince.

fellowship in 1 John 1:3, which is the same word translated *fellowship*[9] in Acts 2:42. This is the Greek word *koinonia*, which means a sharing of all you are and all you have — communication, distribution, and participation. This is the life of faith that the early believers and the apostles shared with Yahshua and the Father.

> *Then those who gladly received his word were baptized; and that day about three thousand souls were added to them. And they continued steadfastly in the apostles' doctrine and fellowship, in the breaking of bread, and in prayers. (Acts 2:41-42)*

Those who walk in the Spirit can and must fulfill the righteous requirements of the Law.

Many had not continued steadfastly in John's teachings and fellowship. They had fallen from the glory the church began with. John explained what this meant in 1 John 2:4, *"He who says, 'I know Him' and does not keep His commandments, is a liar, and the truth is not in him."*

Some may think that keeping His commandments places them under the law. And it is true: trying to keep His commandments without the Holy Spirit would be bondage and legalism. Yet those who walk in the Spirit can and must fulfill the righteous requirements of the law.[10] Others may say, "I obey His commandments and keep His word," but He said this is only possible for those who hate their life in this world, and who come to the place where He is:

> *He who loves his life will lose it, and he who hates his life in this world will keep it for eternal life. If anyone serves Me, let him follow Me; and where I am, there My servant will be also. If anyone serves Me, him My Father will honor. (John 12:25-26)*

When 1 John was read to the church, those who heard it had to judge their walk according to the litmus test of 1 John 1:7 and 1 John 2:6. That is just what we have to do today when we read it: ask ourselves the question, "Do we have fellowship (a common life) with one another because we walk as He walked?" They could not have fellowship with the Savior in heaven without having it with John, their apostle, as well. His letter did not persuade those who were not in fellowship with him. They

---

[9] *Fellowship* is in the Greek a very rich word: (#2842 from 2844); partnership, i.e. (literally) participation, or (social) intercourse, or (pecuniary, which means relating to or involving money) benefaction; (to) communicate, communication, communion, contribution, distribution, fellowship.   [10] Romans 8:1-4

continued to love the world, dispute his teachings, and not meet the needs of their brothers. Such "believers" effectively discarded 1 John as an "epistle of straw."

Martin Luther's condemnation of the Letter of James as just such a worthless epistle (calling it an "epistle of straw") shows how easily this can happen. Luther was upset because it threw a wrench into his gospel of being saved by faith alone, for James wrote "faith without works is dead," and "The religion of a man is worthless who does not bridle his tongue, for instance, or care for the widows and the orphans in his community."[11] Faced with this, Luther, a man famous for his foul tongue and fiery invective, had to make a choice.[12] Was he wrong? Had he himself failed the litmus test James gave him? Or was James wrong, uninspired — a man of the flesh? Like the "stiff-necked" men of old Israel, Luther "stoned the prophet" rather than trembling at his word.

That is why disregarding 1 John as an "epistle of straw" doesn't mean to question its inspiration, authorship, or date of composition. It means to *ignore* (as Martin Luther ignored the Letter of James) the evidence of the litmus test which 1 John gives to all who claim to believe. His sheep hear His voice and do not reason it away, even when He tells them they don't really know Him or His salvation. ✳

---

[11] James 2:14-17 and 1:26, respectively   [12] One example among many by Luther, which directly contradicts James 3:9: "For I am unable to pray without at the same time cursing," Luther said, "If I am prompted to say, 'Hallowed be Thy name,' I must add, 'Cursed, damned, outraged be the name of papists.' Indeed, I pray thus orally every day and in my heart, without intermission" And concerning Catholic clergy he wrote, "The Rhine is scarcely big enough to drown the whole accursed gang of Roman extortioners... cardinals, archbishops, bishops, and abbots." (Quoted in W. Durant, *The Reformation*, p. 418)

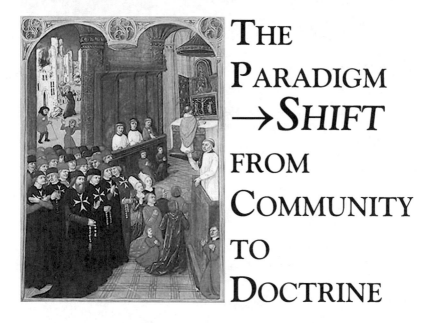

THE PARADIGM →SHIFT FROM COMMUNITY TO DOCTRINE

Beloved, although I was very eager to write to you about our common salvation, I found it necessary to write appealing to you to contend for the faith that was once for all delivered to the saints. (Jude 1:3)

After the first century, right doctrine became the "litmus test" for faith instead of loving as Yahshua[1] commanded.[2] Late in the first century, Jude urged the believers to *contend* for the faith delivered once for all to the saints. This word translated as *faith* means the persuasion to do what the Master commanded, for this was the purpose for the faith the 3000 received by hearing the gospel on the day of Pentecost in Acts 2:36-45.[3] The word *love* was defined by Yahshua in John 14 and 15 in the same terms, "If you love Me, you will keep My commandments,"[4] which is amplified in John 15, "Keep my commandments... just as I have kept My Father's commandments."[5]

Faith, trust, and obedience were the guiding lights of the first disciples, whose faith turned the world upside down.[6] But today the word

---

[1] *Yahshua* is the Hebrew name of the Savior; see *The Name Above All Names* on page 151. [2] John 13:34-35; 1 John 3:14,16,23; 5:12-13 [3] Romans 10:17 where *faith*, #4102 in Strong's Greek Concordance of the New Testament, comes from #3982, which means *persuasion*. The latter word is often translated *trust* in the KJV in places such as Mark 10:24 and Luke 20:6. [4] John 14:15, also verses 21 and 23 strike the same note, a threefold repetition by the Savior of the same theme in just a few words. Obviously obedience was something He considered of vital importance for *His* disciples. [5] John 15:10, which is itself an amplification of some of His first words to His disciples in Matthew 5:17-19 about keeping His Father's word and teaching others to do the same. [6] Acts 17:6 in the KJV.

faith in Jude 1:3 is taken to simply mean the knowledge and assent to religious truths, without regard to good works, which is therefore a false faith.[7] In reality, the only assurance of faith is Ephesians 2:10 and 4:16 — doing the good works one was saved to do in order to build up the Body. These things are the very reason one is saved!

> *For we are His workmanship, created in Christ Jesus for good works, which God prepared beforehand that we should walk in them. (Ephesians 2:10)*

Here is an Amazing Thing!

So Jude 1:3 has nothing whatsoever to do with doctrinal correctness, as the context in verse 4 proves:

> *For certain men have crept in unnoticed, who long ago were marked out for this condemnation, ungodly men, who turn the grace of our God into lewdness and deny the only Master and Lord, Jesus Christ. (Jude 1:4)*

Here Jude speaks of grace being turned into license to do your own thing, doing what is right in your own eyes. This started to overtake the early church when there was no longer true authority from God in the church.[8] There was no restraint; each one did whatever he wanted, but still maintained a form of godliness, although denying its power.

This reveals an amazing thing: doctrine, or the right theology, requires no *faith* to believe.[9] All it takes is mental assent, and all it gives in return is mental confidence. Such "faith" results historically (and currently) in living lives indistinguishable from the surrounding world — living independently rather than together with other believers.[10] In this truly applies the wisdom of the ancients, "He who separates himself seeks his own desire."[11] Yes, true faith is for the purpose of doing the works prepared for one to do in the Body of Messiah, which is the Community of the Redeemed, and which must be just as real and alive as the community in Jerusalem described in Acts 2 and 4.

Theology requires no faith, but John 13:34-35 *does* require faith, for it transcends what any man can do naturally:

> *"A new commandment I give to you, that you love one another; as I have loved you, that you also love one another. By this all will know that you are My disciples, if you have love for one another."*

The Litmus Test

John the Apostle spelled out the true "litmus test" of faith in his first letter. A litmus test decisively proves the presence or absence of a particular ingredient. The litmus test of 1 John reveals the presence or

[7] James 2:14-26   [8] Judges 17:6; 21:25   [9] James 2:19   [10] Acts 2:44
[11] Proverbs 18:1

absence of God's love, which is the evidence of true faith. 1 John 3:14 reveals the truth or falsehood of one's claim to have passed from death into life:

> [14]We know that we have passed from death to life, because we love the brethren. He who does not love his brother abides in death. [16]By this we know love, because He laid down His life for us. And we also ought to lay down our lives for the brethren. [23]And this is His commandment: that we should believe on the name of His Son Jesus Christ and love one another, as He gave us commandment.

1 John 3:16 and 23 also require faith, without which even someone with the right doctrine won't pass the litmus test of 1 John 3:14 — regardless of whether he *says* he believes.[12] Believing the right doctrine requires no faith, no love, and no laying down of one's life for his brothers.

> "I beseech you therefore, brethren, by the mercies of God, that you present your bodies a living sacrifice, holy, acceptable to God, which is your reasonable service. And do not be conformed to this world, but be transformed by the renewing of your mind, that you may prove what is that good and acceptable and perfect will of God." (Romans 12:1-2)

No one can do Romans 12:1 unless he obeys verse 2 by faith as well. Otherwise, the faith of Jude 1:3 is merely doctrine, the theology of theologians, learned men who can quote many scripture verses, but laying down their lives as 1 John 3:16 says is far from them. They can only teach their flocks the same "faith" as they have. A student, when fully trained, will be like his teacher. So their empty "faith" has been passed down ever since theological Bible schools have existed on earth. They have no relationship with the true Messiah[13] and can only foster mental assent to theological terms, concepts, and decrees thought up by the apostates of the fourth century.[14]

The church turned from being the persecuted to being the persecutor.

These apostate leaders valued doctrine higher than love, and three centuries after Messiah's death began persecuting people, deposing bishops, and banishing into exile those considered to have the wrong doctrine. Ultimately, they started killing those they deemed heretics. So why is it always those with the

---

[12] John 5:24   [13] 2 Corinthians 11:4,15   [14] See *The Church Councils of the Emperor* at *http://theblackboxspeaks.org/church-councils.html*

right doctrine who end up killing those with the wrong doctrine? They obviously didn't understand 1 Corinthians 1:10 in the right spirit:

> Now I plead with you, brethren, by the name of our Lord Jesus Christ, that you all speak the same thing, and that there be no divisions among you, but that you be perfectly joined together in the same mind and in the same judgment.

Paul is pleading for the brothers in Corinth to be in unity; he is pleading in the very name by which they were saved. He is *pleading*, not *forcing* — you can't force unity. Forced unity is not the right spirit. As 2 Corinthians 11:4,13-15 clearly states, only Satan's servants or ministers could ever do what the Christian theologians did to dissenters. All this was in absolute violation of the Master's words to leave them alone, to let them be.[15]

The reason Jude so urgently said to *contend* for the faith that was imparted in the beginning was because he saw change coming in — a terrible change away from the pattern in Acts 2 and 4 and toward what would become the state church of Constantine. We can see the change in the way Christians thought, being persuaded and influenced by a different spirit, propagated by a different gospel, and ending up with a different Jesus from the one they accepted in the beginning.[16]

---

[15] John 12:47-48; Luke 9:54-55, NKJV; Acts 5:34-39, and the apostle Paul's words in 1 Corinthians 5:12-13.   [16] 2 Corinthians 11:2-4; Galatians 1:6-7

The Tragedy of Christian History

Starting with their acceptance by Emperor Constantine, the church turned from being the *persecuted* to being the *persecutor*. But by that time, the Holy Spirit had long ago left the church.[17] No longer could anyone truthfully confess that Messiah "is come in the flesh" at their church, since it was no longer a community where all things were held in common.[18] Neither could anyone say from his *experience* that he served the Savior *where He is*,[19] but only from his mind. As the church declined in its love in every place,[20] in spite of Paul's exhortation to them in Ephesians to love Messiah with an undying, incorruptible love,[21]

What was the final outcome of the shift from love to doctrine? Killing those with "bad" doctrine.

none seemed to be able to pass the litmus test of 1 John 5:13. This was because active, real, sacrificial love of one's brothers and sisters was no longer the emphasis,[22] but rather mental assent to a list of doctrines now called "The Faith." So this doctrinal "faith" replaced the works true faith was meant to energize, as James later wrote in the second century.[23]

So very early on, as the church careened down its fatal decline, the emphasis shifted to doctrinal correctness, which is now considered the evidence of faith. But Jude, who wrote by the end of the first century, looking into the second, urged that they *contend* or have a vigorous defense of the faith delivered once and for all to God's people. What he meant by this was the faith that produced the expression of the abundant life recorded in Acts 2 and 4. That was "the faith once for all delivered to the saints."[24] But faith only came to those who had ears to hear.[25]

When love left, the Holy Spirit left, and the light (the lampstands in each place) was extinguished.[26] Eventually those who were as John 9:41 describes took the word *contend* in Jude 1:3 to mean taking up arms to force their "right doctrine" upon those with "wrong doctrine" under pain

---

[17] Revelation 2:4-5   [18] 1 John 4:2-3   [19] John 12:25-6   [20] 1 Corinthians 1:2
[21] Ephesians 6:24   [22] 1 John 3:16 and 23   [23] James 1:26-27; 2:14-26
[24] Acts 2:44-45   [25] Acts 2:40; John 18:37; 10:27   [26] Revelation 2:4-5

of death. This was contrary to the words of the true Messiah, "My kingdom is not of this world. If my kingdom were of this world, my servants would fight."[27]

The "Sign" of Sanctification

Jude echoed the Apostle Paul's words in 1 Corinthians 1:2 in the opening of his epistle, when he wrote to the few who were not yet disqualified:

> To those who are called, sanctified [set apart] in God the Father and kept for Jesus Christ: May mercy, peace, and love be multiplied to you. (Jude 1:1-2)

This sanctification was to be an obvious sign of God's set apart people in the New Covenant *just as it was to have been in the Old.* They were to be separated by God's purifying work in their lives from the lust and greed and anger and hatred of the world around them. And the sign of this sanctification, both within and without this new Israel, was still the Sabbath, as the writer to the Hebrews made clear:

> There remains therefore a sabbath-keeping for the people of God [i.e., for those who enter God's rest]. (Hebrews 4:9)

So Jude's words were addressed to those who were *still* set apart by God the Father, and kept for Messiah. May mercy and peace and love be multiplied to you, who are *sanctified* as in 1 Corinthians 1:2. At that time there were still those separated from the world in the Body of Messiah, the Community, as in Acts 2:42-47 and 4:32-37. They were set apart in a *place* where the refining process can take place in each one's life, which cannot be accomplished unless one is separated from fellowship with the world in that place where Messiah actually dwells in His Body.[28] The Sabbath was like a sign over each place where God was sanctifying His people:

> Speak also to the children of Israel, saying: "Surely My Sabbaths you shall keep, for it is a sign between Me and you throughout your generations, that you may know that I am the LORD who sanctifies you." (Exodus 31:13)

In 1 Corinthians 1:2, "in every place" means in every township where God's name had been caused to dwell by the direct process of John 13:20 — "He who receives whomever I send receives Me; and he who receives Me receives Him who sent Me." Starting from Jerusalem, the first community swarmed to surrounding towns in Judea, and it was according to this "Judean pattern" that Paul modeled the communities he established.[29] Of course, it was "with persecutions," as Mark 10:29-30

---

[27] John 18:36   [28] John 12:26   [29] 1 Thessalonians 2:14

promises. This is the mark of those who have separated themselves in a place in which they can be made pure as 1 John 3:1-3, "That they may see Him as He is, and everyone who has this hope in them purifies himself as He is pure."[30]

Mark 10:29-30 was the Master's answer to His disciples' question, "Who then can be saved?"[31] It is the answer never given by Christian preachers today. Verse 27 explains how one is saved by *obedience to His gospel,* thus proving they have been persuaded to do His will. Someone has to receive the faith to not only believe in Him, but to do what He required of all whom He would save from this present evil world. Their obedience to the gospel would put them into a place where they could be purified — *where He is.*[32] There, and only there, can anyone serve Him. As 1 Corinthians 1:2 implies, it must be a set-apart place that is in the world but not of it.[33] This takes a *community* in a township where disciples daily love and encourage one another.[34]

The word *sanctify* in John 17:17 is the same as in 1 Corinthians 1:2 — set apart from the evil world system to be made ready (prepared) to rule with Messiah; and John 17:18 is their mission. This is why, several centuries later, the influential leaders of the church could cheerfully go along with Constantine (who was both an unbeliever and the head of the pagan Roman state religion) endorsing their religion. He offered the church worldly acceptance in place of persecution. *Everything* radically changed when the church accepted his proposal.

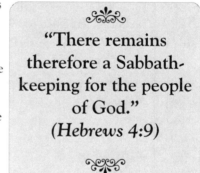

"There remains therefore a Sabbath-keeping for the people of God."
(*Hebrews* 4:9)

In 321 AD, Constantine effectively took down the sign of the Sabbath. The mission of the church had changed in the minds of both its leaders and its people. No longer was it called to set people apart from the world. No, much rather it was now called to send people *into the world* to be judges, governing officials, soldiers,[35] and in time powerful political leaders, even rulers. Friendship with the world became a sign of friendship with God, in sharp contrast to the wisdom of James 4:1-3. This is why the church could now "rest" on the day of the Sun god (Sunday), for *his* domain is truly the kingdoms and affairs of this world.

---

[30] Romans 5:3-5; 2 Peter 1:4-11; 1 Peter 5:4 [31] Mark 10:26 [32] John 12:25-26
[33] John 17:14-17 [34] Hebrews 3:13 and 10:24-26 [35] By the end of the fourth century it was difficult to find a soldier who *wasn't* a Christian. By 416 AD, non-Christians were forbidden to serve in the army! See *Codex Theodosianus XVI* x. 21 (*http://www.sfts.edu/ocker/hs1080/paganlaw.htm*).

Who then can be Saved?

One would think, reading Christian history, that worldly success and national power are the hallmarks of true faith, contrary to the teachings and example of Yahshua. But the fact is, shocking as it may seem, that for someone to walk down the aisle in the Billy Graham Crusade and be "saved" is impossible. He goes back home and does the very same things as before, except now supposedly he's going to heaven when he dies, as if that were all the Savior gave up His life for. If you want to see what He *really* paid such a high price for, consider how the church was in the beginning, when all who believed were together. Read about those days with open eyes and an open heart.

So then, hasn't this "sincere believer" at the Billy Graham Crusade simply believed in vain, as those in John 2:23-25? Was it not only make believe? "Might as well make believe" you love Him, which is to say you do but not obey Him.[36] But this is not what the Master told His disciples they had to do in order to be saved.[37]

"Who then can be saved?" they asked. Only those who hear and obey the gospel, including the "many other words" (the "hard sayings of Christ") as in Acts 2:36-41 and Mark 10:17-30. The "rich young ruler" wanted to know what he had to do to be saved. The answer is the same now as it was for the 3,000 on the day of Pentecost, who gave up everything in response to the first message of salvation which the apostles preached in obedience to Messiah's commission.[38] Ask yourself why the preaching of the gospel today doesn't produce the same results. Could it be a different gospel?[39] ✤

---

[36] John 14:15,21; 1 John 2:4   [37] Mark 10:17-30   [38] Matthew 28:19-20
[39] 2 Corinthians 11:4

THE RESTORATION
OF ALL THINGS

*Yahshua prophesied that before His return
there would be a restoration of all things cast aside
by the fallen religious system, which has made
a mockery of His name.
There must be a people raised up on the earth
to make His name great among the nations,
so that He can return
and bring judgment to this earth.*

*The articles in this section
speak of the things that are now being restored
by those who love Him enough to surrender
their own lives and possessions for His cause.
This includes His true name, Yahshua,
and His identity as a man who overcame
every temptation in order to be our sinless sacrifice.
And it also includes the communal life
of love and unity that demonstrates
the power of His resurrection.*

A MUSTARD SEED

Not so impressive to the natural eye...

There is so much spoken about the Kingdom of God in the New Testament, it's amazing. One of the very first times Yahshua spoke, He spoke about the Kingdom of God.[1] It says, "It's right at the door! The Kingdom is right here! It's at hand!" And of course, all the Jews were looking for the Kingdom that was going to come and rout out the Roman Empire and establish Messiah's rule on the earth. That's what they were thinking He was talking about. Yahshua said, "It's right at hand," but of course two thousand years later, it still hasn't happened. But what He was talking about was the community He was going to establish by His Holy Spirit, which would be His reign in people's lives in the midst of a darkened world.

You can see that there are two manifestations of the Kingdom; the one now is like the mustard seed. We're like a mustard seed that's so tiny you can hardly see it. It's hardly observable. The birds of the air and the tiny field mice can hardly see it. It's so small, but it gets larger and larger and larger as it grows. It's not so observable, that Kingdom we're a part of, which will bring in the Millennial Kingdom when Yahshua returns to this earth. Then it will be totally observable. It will be a sudden display of the power of God.

So Yahshua talked about the mustard seed in Matthew 13:31-33, how it falls to the ground unnoticed even by the birds and the mice and any other creature that would want to steal that seed. The seed sprouts up into a bush, and grows and grows so large that it's greater than all the plants in the garden. It's the biggest one. And all the birds of the air can nest in its branches — all the birds of different feathers, as it speaks about in Ezekiel 17:23. When that tree grows, all the birds of every feather, meaning different nationalities, cultures, and races, will come and dwell

---

[1] Mark 1:14-15

together in that one tree in one brand new culture and nation.

That is unheard of today. One kind of bird will occupy one tree and another the other tree, but they won't mix together. But in the last days, they will dwell together. People from all different cultures will come together to be a part of that one new culture.[2] That is contrary to fallen nature. In the natural world they can't live together. But we who believe will be able to live together, and that will be the greatest witness that the heavenly Father has done something in the hearts of men — that we can come out of that fatally flawed society and live together in peace.

So it begins small, and people even scorn it, but against all odds it grows and spreads throughout the world. And that mighty tree will bring healing and shelter to all the depressed and lonely people — all the people out there who need a home. He makes a home for the lonely.[3] In Luke 17:20, the Pharisees were asking, "Is the kingdom going to come?" Yahshua replied, *"The Kingdom of God does not come with observation. Nor will people say, 'Here it is,' or 'There it is,' because the Kingdom of God is among you."*

The Kingdom of God certainly wasn't within them (as some translations read), for He was talking to the Pharisees. It is properly translated, "among you," as in the Living Bible, or "in your midst," as in the NASB. The translators missed the whole point, for the kingdom that He's talking about doesn't come about noticeably or suddenly, with power and great armies. No! It comes "without observation." The Pharisees didn't even know that the Kingdom of God was in their midst. They were asking for the Kingdom of God and Yahshua said, "The kingdom is among you right now!"

It's just like the people around us today — they don't understand that the Kingdom of God is in their midst. They may see a people living together who seemingly like one another, and are a little bit different, and they seem peaceful. But what they are seeing is just a tiny little seed growing. It's growing and growing, little by little, but it's not so observable

---

[2] Galations 3:28; 1 Peter 2:9-10   [3] Psalm 68:5-6

yet, not as it will be when the consummation of the age comes, after we have proclaimed the Gospel of the Kingdom as a witness.[4] We will have declared it by the witness of our life, by our living together just like Acts 2:44. And as we continued to grow, colonize, swarm, and spread all over the earth, then people were able to observe our behavior[5] more and more.

But now, we are struggling to even survive. It's against all odds that this mustard seed will sprout. But if it sprouts, even though from the tiniest seed, it becomes the biggest tree in the garden, and all the birds of different feathers will gather in its branches.

The kingdom doesn't come suddenly. It starts with the smallest seed. But that seed is still in the midst of all the people in each locality as it grows and grows. One might think the kingdom isn't coming, but it's as in Yahshua's day: the kingdom was in their midst and they didn't know it.

The apostles said in Acts 1:6, "Is this the time that the kingdom which will rule the entire earth is going to come?"[6] But He said, "It's not for you to know." It was not for them to know, because Daniel is a sealed book, and its unsealing has to wait until the time of the end.[7] We know that in the very end of days, knowledge will increase and men will travel to and fro.[8] Knowledge will increase *exponentially* and become instantly available. Probably in those days, two thousand years ago, they thought they were in the last days because they had the Roman roads to travel on, but it is speaking of an *exponential* increase.

So it says in Luke 17:20 that the kingdom does not come so that it is so apparent. It comes as the mustard seed — *stealthily*, which means to bring to pass in a not-so-observable manner. It unfolds a little at a time. It just sneaks in there and grows. No one really knows. Even the governments don't know what's going on. If they knew this was the Stone Kingdom of Daniel's prophecy that is going to destroy all the governments and kings of the earth, they might do something about us (but God would just laugh at them, as Psalm 2:4 says). But it is growing stealthily. It is right in the midst of them and they don't even know it.

When Yahshua comes back, it's going to be a grand event, but now the emergence of the kingdom is not such a grand event. Right now it's just little, humble us, and we gather people as Daniel 2:44-45 says — a "stone" cut from the mountain of the world without human hands.

The first message Yahshua preached was that the Kingdom of God was at hand. But they were thinking, "The Messiah is coming to take over the world." But the people of Israel were totally rebellious at that point in their history. They felt as if they could just be given the kingdom right then, but they didn't deserve it. Yahshua said, "I'm going to take the kingdom away from you and give it to a nation who will produce the fruit

---

[4] Matthew 24:14 [5] 1 Peter 2:12 [6] Daniel 2:35 [7] Daniel 12:9; 2:44-45
[8] Daniel 12:4

of it. Since you didn't produce the fruit, I'm going to give it to a nation who will!"[9]

That's why Paul said that "our twelve tribes who serve God night and day" will do it *for* them,[10] because we are here in their place, doing what they didn't do.[11] We do it for them in order that in the next age they can have the land that God promised to Abraham when He walked through the split animals as if to say, "Let it be that if I don't give you this enemy-free land, I'll be cursed Myself."[12] He made a self-cursing oath. So there has to be a people who will carry it out for Him by His grace.

It says in Matthew 12:50, "Whoever *does* the will of my Father in heaven is my brother, my sister, and my mother." If you look up the word *does*, there is a great definition. It means to carry it out, to cause or make it happen. That is the one who *does* the will of our Father in heaven.[13] No one can do that except by being in the Body of Messiah, which has to be restored on the face of the earth.

Two Aspects of the Kingdom

We have to understand about the two aspects of the Kingdom. The apostles said, "Is it us? Is the Kingdom going to come now? Are you going to return and establish the Kingdom in our lifetime?" They thought He was going to usher in the Kingdom after He rose from the dead. But Matthew 24:14 was a long ways off — two thousand years ahead, and they couldn't fathom that. Yahshua would have discouraged them if He had said, "No, you are all going to fall away." But Paul wondered whether he had labored in vain, though he knew he would have his reward.[14]

People lost their first love and became scattered and divided. And we may see similar things going on in our midst, but we can't lose heart because we know the threshing floor has got to be cleared out. It's only the true wheat that will remain. All the chaff has got to be blown away because the chaff has no glory. But the wheat has glory; it has weight. You throw it up in the air and the chaff will blow away, but the wheat falls down at Yahshua's feet.

So it says *does* in Matthew 12:50. It's not the one who mentally *believes*, but the one who *does*. Faith without works is dead. *Does* speaks of a *doer* — one who takes an active part in bringing about what Yahshua told us to pray for in Matthew 6:9-11. We need to pray, "Father, I want your will to be done!" And who is going to do it? Someone has got to do His will, and whoever *does* it, that's His family. That's His brother and

---

[9] Matthew 21:43; 1 Peter 2:9   [10] Acts 26:7 in the Williams New Testament "...which promise our twelve tribes, by devotedly worshiping day and night, hope to see fulfilled for them. It is for this hope, your Majesty, that I am accused by some Jews." Genesis 18:19   [11] Genesis 15:18   [12] Genesis 15:8-21; Jeremiah 34:18-20   [13] Matthew 7:21; Ephesians 6:6; Hebrews 10:36; James 1:25; 1 Peter 4:2; 1 John 2:17; 3:22   [14] Galatians 4:11; Philippians 2:14-16; 1 Thessalonians 3:5

sister and mother. If we're not praying for it, we're certainly not going to do it. Only those who are praying for it will do it.

So the word *does* is speaking of the one who carries out His will, who brings it about, who does it deliberately, knowing what he's doing. He causes or produces an effect, bringing it into existence. At first it's not so glorious, not so impressive to the natural eye.

Mysteries of the Kingdom

That's what Yahshua said in Matthew 13:11, "The mysteries of the Kingdom of Heaven have been revealed to you, but not to others." The kingdom that's now forming will become a great mountain that will  fill the whole earth.[15] There are not two kingdoms — a kingdom now and then a kingdom to come. There's only one kingdom, and it turns into a great and mighty kingdom that governs the whole world.

Right now we're not political at all. We're not involved in the world's governments, but in the next age it will all be the Kingdom of Yahshua. It will be a great and mighty kingdom as it talks about in Daniel 2:34-35. The stone, formed in this age, becomes a great mountain and fills the whole earth. As the parable in Matthew 13:33 says, the woman puts the yeast in her dough and it permeates the whole lump. Just a little leaven leavens the whole loaf, which is the whole world. But it is not in this age, but in the next age.

Yahshua spoke all these parables using similes and metaphors, and they can be so confusing in our minds. He spoke in so many figures of speech — about farming, fishing, women baking bread, and merchants buying pearls, and so much more. We have to consider it. It's only given to His disciples to understand it. The natural mind can't comprehend it. It's the secret, the mystery of the Kingdom.

Resistible or Irresistible?

The Kingdom that is going to come will be irresistible, but the Kingdom now is resistible. You can resist it if you want to; you can shun it. God made it that way because He only wants the pure heart of man. He doesn't want anything except a pure, loving heart for our Creator. Those are the only people who are going to bring in that Kingdom — those who love Him with all their heart, soul, and strength.

---

[15] Daniel 2:35

So the Kingdom now is resistible. The men of the earth can resist it. But the day will come when they won't be able to resist it. It's going to come and flatten everything out. Then Yahshua will reign supreme, and we'll rule with Him over the nations – on the earth and then the universe.[16]

Our Father is going to have His will done by a people who do His will in this age. We may think we can just say, "Father, your will be done." When I was young, I had to pray it in school every day. But we didn't have an iota of understanding about it. It was just something we memorized. But when we pray, "Father, your will be done," that means, "Give us the power and the strength and the grace to do it, to bring it about." That's what it means. "Deliver us from the evil one."

All those who are falling into sin are not praying to be delivered from evil. They could care less about His Kingdom. They aren't praying to be delivered. If we pray to be delivered from evil, do you think our Father is not going to deliver us? Of course, He's going to deliver us! That's what He wants to do! If we say, "Deliver us from evil" and evil comes upon us, what is that? It doesn't make sense.

We're chosen as Abraham was chosen. All the seed of Abraham are chosen. Why are we chosen? We are chosen that we would command our children.[17] Parents are to command their children or they're not the seed of Abraham. And the children are to be commandable. And the outcome of that is to bring about what God had promised Abraham. We have to bring about the promise of the enemy-free land for Abraham's natural offspring. Then the Kingdom will come and be established in the next age, and all the apostles will sit on thrones judging the twelve tribes of Israel in the next age.[18] Who's going to bring it about? It's not going to just happen out of the blue. It's going to take a people who will put all of Yahshua's enemies under His feet[19] and crush the head of the serpent. ✤

---

[16] Revelation 21:24; 22:2 [17] Genesis 18:19 [18] Matthew 19:28
[19] Hebrews 10:13; Acts 3:21; Romans 16:20

THE NAME ABOVE ALL NAMES

In the days of John the Baptist and the Son of God, the preserved language of the devout Jews was Hebrew. So, when the angel Gabriel brought the good news to the Hebrew virgin, Miriam (or *Mary* in English), that she would give birth to the Savior of the world, and told her what His name would be, what language do you suppose he spoke? Hebrew, of course! And certainly Miriam and Yoceph (or *Joseph* in English) named the child just as the angel had commanded them — *Yahshua*.

In Matthew 1:21, your Bible probably reads, "…and you shall call His name Jesus, for He will save His people from their sins." But the name *Jesus* is a modern English adaptation of the Greek name, *Iesous*, which is itself a corruption of the original Hebrew name *Yahshua*. The name *Jesus* or *Iesous* has no meaning of its own, but the Hebrew name *Yahshua* literally means *Yahweh's Salvation*,[1] which makes sense out of what the angel said in Matthew 1:21, "…you shall call His name Yahshua [*Yahweh's Salvation*], for He shall save His people from their sins."

If you look in an old King James Bible, you will find the name *Jesus* in these two passages:

> *Which also our fathers that came after brought in with* **Jesus** *into the possession of the Gentiles, whom God drave out before the face of our fathers, unto the days of David…* (Acts 7:45, KJV)

> *For if* **Jesus** *had given them rest, then would he not afterward have spoken of another day.* (Hebrews 4:8, KJV)

However, if you look in any modern translation of the Bible, including the New King James, you will find that in place of the name *Jesus* they use the name *Joshua*, for in the context it is clear that it is speaking there of Moses' successor and not the Son of God. But in the Greek manuscript the name in both of these verses is *Iesous*.

You see, *Joshua* is the popular English transliteration of the Hebrew name *Yahshua*. Joshua of the Old Testament had the same name as the One called *Jesus* in the New Testament, for Joshua was the prophetic forerunner of the Son of God, bringing Israel into the Promised Land and leading them to victory over their enemies. But since the translators

---

[1] *Yah* is the personal name of God, and *shua* is from a Hebrew root word that means "to save." God identified Himself to Moses as *YAH* (meaning "I AM") in Exodus 3:14, as in Psalm 68:4 ("whose name is *Yah*"), and as most familiar in the word Hallelu*yah* ("Praise *Yah*"). And in John 5:43 and 17:11, Yahshua says that He came in His Father's name, "the name which You have given Me" (NASB), so it is not surprising that the Father's name would be incorporated into the Son's name, *Yahshua*.

obviously know this fact, why do they only translate *Iesous* as *Joshua* in these two verses, and as *Jesus* everywhere else?

The NIV New Testament even has a footnote supporting this fact under Matthew 1:21: "*Jesus* is the Greek form of *Joshua*."

But the fact is, the name of God's Son was not even written or pronounced as "Jesus" in English until the 1600s, simply because there was no "J" sound or letter in English before then.[2] The modern letter "J" evolved from the letter "I" which began to be written with a "tail" when it appeared as the first letter in a word. So in old English the name now written as *Jesus* was actually written and pronounced much like the original Greek *Iesous*.

A page from the 1611 Authorized Version (King James Bible). Note the lack of a "J" in the Savior's name.

Eventually the hard "J" sound crept into the English language to accompany the different way of writing the initial "I" in the name.

You may also find it interesting that in Acts 26:14-15, it says that the apostle Paul heard the name of the Son of God pronounced "in the Hebrew tongue" by the Son of God Himself, so he certainly didn't hear the Greek name *Iesous* or the English name *Jesus*, but rather the Hebrew name, the name above all names, *Yahshua*.[3] ❧

---

[2] *Compact Edition of the Oxford English Dictionary* (Oxford University Press, 1971), pp. 1496,1507   [3] Philippians 2:9; Acts 4:1 2

You brood of vipers! Who warned you to flee from the wrath to come? thundered Yochanan, son of Zechariah, as he stood waist-deep in the Jordan River and watched the religious leaders of Israel gather on the riverbank.[1] It wasn't what they wanted to hear, nor were they expecting it. After all, they were God's people, weren't they? So why this scathing rebuke?

THE UNSHAKABLE CERTAINTY

It was obvious to Yochanan that the ax was already laid at the root of their fruitless branches — the time for reform had passed. The tree was dead, and Yochanan had been born for the very purpose of pronouncing it so, and preparing the way for the Messiah, as his father had prophesied,

> *"And you, child, will be called the prophet of the Most High; for you will go before the Lord to prepare his ways, to give knowledge of salvation to his people in the forgiveness of their sins, because of the tender mercy of our God, whereby the sunrise shall visit us from on high to give light to those who sit in darkness and in the shadow of death, to guide our feet into the way of peace."* (Luke 1:76-79, ESV)

Zechariah, an aged priest at the time of his son's birth, had known well the condition of Israel. His people were in dire need of salvation, for in spite of their great heritage they were sitting in darkness and the shadow of death. His heart ached for his people. And in the thirty years since he had spoken those words, the darkness of their fallen religion had only increased. How Zechariah's heart would have pounded if he could have seen and heard his son that day.

But when Yochanan saw Yahshua[2] of Nazareth, whom he knew to be the Messiah, coming down the riverbank toward him to be baptized, his confidence was shaken. Who was he to baptize the Messiah? His objection received only the cryptic response, "Permit it at this time; for in

---

[1] Matthew 3:1-17 is one account of the ministry of the man commonly called "John the Baptist." [2] *Yahshua* is the Hebrew name which is commonly rendered as *Jesus* in English. See page 151 for a more in-depth explanation.

this way it is fitting for us to fulfill all righteousness." At that, he immersed Yahshua into the muddy waters, and as He emerged, Yochanan saw what appeared to be a dove alight upon Him, and heard a voice from heaven saying, "You are My beloved Son, in whom I am well pleased."[3]

Why did the Messiah Himself need to be baptized? And why did the Father speak those words audibly to His Son as soon as He emerged from the waters? The answers to these questions touch the very nature and purpose of the Son of God — His humanity and divinity. In past centuries many have died over questions such as these, and even today there are some who would call for our blood, if they could, for writing what you are about to read. But for those who love the truth, these words will ring true and answer some of the deepest questions of your heart.

God or Man?

It is a well-established doctrine in Christianity that Jesus is both fully God and fully Man, but what exactly does this mean? What are the practical implications for those who look to Him as their Savior? Most of us have grown up with the image of baby Jesus with a halo on his head, and pictures of a striking, handsome adult Jesus. Even the typical pictures of the crucifixion show a fair-skinned, unblemished man with a little slit in his side and a placid expression on his face. Who can identify with such a Jesus, so beautiful in his perfection, unaffected by sufferings?

But the scriptures give quite a different picture. They tell of a man who was physically unimpressive,[4] the son of a poor Hebrew woman,[5] who for most of His life worked as a carpenter.[6] Although He was miraculously conceived, few people took notice of this fact. And although there are fanciful things written about Him in apocryphal writings, the Bible gives only a small but essential glimpse of His upbringing.

His family had gone to Jerusalem for the Passover and discovered on their way home that Yahshua was not in their company. Evidently He was a trusted son whom they assumed was serving in some way amongst their caravan, perhaps helping care for the animals. They returned to Jerusalem and searched for several days before they found Him in the Temple, amazing the teachers with His understanding of the scriptures. He seemed surprised that they hadn't known where to find Him, and they were equally surprised by His question, "Did you not know that I must be about my Father's business?"

Although His parents knew that He was destined to be the Messiah of Israel, clearly they did not expect Him to come into that role so young, nor did they understand what it entailed. But this brief snapshot of His life shows His fascination with the scriptures and how He gave Himself to

---

[3] Mark 1:11; Luke 3:22   [4] Isaiah 53:2-3   [5] Luke 2:24 shows that Joseph and Mary gave the offering permitted in the Law (Leviticus 12:8) for those who were too poor to offer a lamb.   [6] Mark 6:3

the task of understanding them. This story begins and ends with two similar statements that show a progression taking place:

> *And the child grew and became strong in spirit, filled with wisdom; and the grace of God was upon Him. … And Jesus increased in wisdom and stature, and in favor with God and men. (Luke 2:40,52)*

Yahshua was not born with the awareness of who He was or what lay ahead of Him. He was born a human baby just like any other healthy baby, except for two invisible qualities: first, that He had not inherited Adam's fallen nature,[7] and second, that His human spirit was one with the divine Spirit.[8] Neither of these differences from the rest of humanity would be readily apparent, however, in a newborn baby. The effects of the Fall take time to be manifested in human babies, and the soul's awareness of the spiritual realm also takes time to develop. So although He must certainly have been a remarkably peaceful baby, He was yet a baby, with a baby's soul — intellect, will, and emotions. From that point He grew, both physically and in the maturity of His soul.

Soul and Spirit

Human beings are spiritual creatures. A man's soul is like the sails on a ship, designed to be filled with a spirit just as a ship's sails are filled with the wind, so as to propel his life on a course. The human spirit (distinct from the soul) was designed as his vital connection to the Spirit of man's Creator, the means by which man (male and female) could orient his soul so as to be filled with that Spirit. Adam was created with this vital connection intact, with the infinite potential of having his soul (intellect,

---

[7] The ovum in Mary's womb had been fertilized by a preserved pure human seed, untainted by the fall of Adam, miraculously implanted in her womb by God. This is implied by Luke 1:35, and confirmed in 1 Corinthians 15:45, where the apostle Paul calls Yahshua the second or last *Adam*. Just as the first Adam was created sinless, so the second Adam was born in that same pure state, unaffected by the first Adam's fall. [8] The eternally existing Word of God (John 1:1), who is one with the Father and the Holy Spirit, was "enfleshed" (John 1:14) in the human body prepared for Him (Hebrews 10:5) in Mary's womb. This is the miracle called *incarnation*. In John 18:37, Yahshua spells it out: "For this cause I was born, and for this cause I have come into the world…" A human son *was born*, and in the same event, the eternally existing, divine Word of God *came into the world* to dwell in that human son.

will, and emotions) fully available to his Creator so as to fulfill his created purpose. But when Adam fell, that vital connection was severed. Man's spirit lay dormant, and his soul lay vulnerable to whatever spirit he was exposed to, just like a ship adrift in the sea.

There are both good and evil spirits at large on the earth. The good spirits have commonly been called *angels*, while the bad have been called *demons*. They are both normally invisible; just like the wind, their presence can only be discerned by their effect. Most people are not sensitive enough to realize when they are being propelled by a spirit, and some even deny their very existence. But spiritual creature that he is, a man's soul is always being affected by spiritual forces. Fortunately, he has a conscience by which he instinctively knows good from evil. The conscience is like a compass by which a man can orient his "ship" so as to spill an errant wind from his sails, or to fill them with a fair breeze, according to where he wants his life to go, or what effect he wants it to have on others. But the tragic reality is that man's fallen inclination to satisfy his short-sighted selfish desires makes him at best an imperfect helmsman and at worst a menace to all afloat on the "sea" of life. As a result, all men's souls are ravaged and in eternal peril.

Son of Man and Son of God

Enter the Son of Man, conceived by means of an unfallen human seed and possessor of a human spirit vitally connected, indeed fused together with the Spirit of His heavenly Father. His soul, as it developed and matured, was always sensitive to that Spirit, fully yielding to the divine Word within Him. It was not that He had no choice in the matter. He had a free human will with which He had to make choices, just as any human being. He had to face the temptations common to all men, and overcome them by the strength of His communion with His Father. The writer of the letter to the Hebrews repeatedly emphasizes this fact:

> *Inasmuch then as the children have partaken of flesh and blood, He Himself likewise shared in the same… Therefore, in all things He had to be made like His brethren, that He might be a merciful and faithful High Priest in things pertaining to God, to make propitiation for the sins of the people. For in that He Himself has suffered, being tempted, He is able to aid those who are tempted. (Hebrews 2:14-18)*

> *For we do not have a high priest who is unable to sympathize with our weaknesses, but one who in every respect has been tempted as we are, yet without sin. (Hebrews 4:15)*

> *In the days of His flesh, Jesus offered up prayers and supplications, with loud cries and tears, to Him who was able to save Him from death, and He was heard because of His reverent submission. Although He was a*

son, He learned obedience through what He suffered. And being made perfect, He became the source of eternal salvation to all who obey Him… (Hebrews 5:7-9)

These verses are meaningless if He was not fully human, having a free will by which He could choose to obey or disobey both His earthly parents and His heavenly Father. It says He *learned obedience* through what He suffered. It does not mean that He was ever rebellious and had to suffer the consequences, for He did not ever sin, but His obedience was perfected as He gave Himself to it. It was not an effortless matter for Him to overcome temptation. All His life, from His childhood until the day He died, He suffered greatly to make the right choices, to deny what would be pleasant or comfortable to His flesh when it was in conflict with the will of His earthly parents as a child, or His heavenly Father as an adult. As a child, the temptations that came to Him and the suffering required to resist them were those common to children. But as He grew up, the temptations were greater and the suffering greater. He increased in His capacity to give Himself to the suffering and surrender His will to His Father's will.[9] This was the *learning*[10] that prepared Him for the greatest suffering of all — the cross and the agonies of death. It was out of love that He gave Himself to His suffering.

> ᕲᕲᕲᕲᕲ
> **Yahshua had to face the temptations common to all men, and overcome them by the strength of His communion with His Father in heaven.**
> ᕲᕲᕲᕲᕲ

For the Joy Set before Him

The Spirit that was in Him bonded Him to the heart of His Father and gave Him the courage and determination to fulfill His purpose. But just as overcoming temptation wasn't automatic for Him, neither was it automatic or effortless for Him to understand who He was or the cause for which He was born. He began life as a human baby, and His mind at birth was ready and waiting to be filled, just as that of any other human baby. He did not have a "crystal ball" with which to see into the future. Even in the last days of His time on earth He did not know the day or the hour when He would return; only the Father knew that.[11] But what He clearly did know by that time was "everything in the Scriptures concerning Himself."[12]

---

[9] Matthew 26:39; Luke 22:42   [10] The Greek word translated as *learned* means to increase; to learn by use and practice.   [11] Matthew 24:36; Mark 13:32; Acts 1:7
[12] Luke 24:27

Yahweh, the God of Israel, very carefully selected the best possible mother and foster-father to raise His Son. He chose the most humble and most spiritual man and woman from the line of David out of the small remnant who were truly "waiting for the consolation of Israel."[13] He sent His chief messenger, the angel Gabriel, to prepare both Miriam and Yoceph[14] for the responsibility that was being given to them, making it perfectly clear to them that this miraculously conceived child entrusted to them was destined to be the Messiah.[15]

But far from being puffed up or boastful about their Son's destiny, they quietly shouldered the awesome responsibility to raise Him in a way that would help prepare Him for that destiny. Surely they filled Him with the stories of their people: of the faith of Abraham and the promise made to him; of his sacrifice of Isaac; of Jacob and his twelve sons; of their deliverance from Egypt; of Moses and the Law; of the Levitical priesthood, the tabernacle and the sacrifices; of the crossing of the Jordan and the conquest of Canaan; of the judges and kings of Israel; of the words of the prophets and the consequences of not heeding them, and of course the wisdom of the Proverbs. And surely as Yahshua learned to read the scriptures for Himself, He filled His soul with them, praying earnestly for the wisdom and insight to understand their meaning, struggling to know who He was and what the prophets had spoken of Him. The divine Spirit in Him revealed to Him who He was very gradually as He matured and as He earnestly sought to know His Father's heart and mind. That is how the Spirit is with all His own people — He hides Himself so that they will diligently seek Him, just as King David taught his son Solomon:

> *"As for you, my son Solomon, know the God of your father, and serve Him with a loyal heart and with a willing mind; for the LORD searches all hearts and understands all the intent of the thoughts. If you seek Him, He will be found by you; but if you forsake Him, He will cast you off forever."* (1 Chronicles 28:9)

Yahshua also observed the troubling realities of life among His people. He saw the grinding poverty of many, and the callous disregard of it by the wealthy few who were often among the religious elite. He saw the lame and blind animals the merchants were selling in the temple courts, and observed who bought them. He took note of the long and pretentious public prayers of the Pharisees, and the humble masses of the common people, like sheep without a shepherd, longing to be led out of the futility of their lives.

Set like Flint

Compassion for His people and the compelling urgency of the Word of God welled up in His soul in steadily increasing measure and clarity

---

[13] Luke 2:25 [14] "Mary and Joseph" in English. [15] Luke 1:32-33; Matthew 1:21

over the years that He labored as a carpenter in Galilee, waiting for the fullness of time. When He heard that Yochanan had begun preaching in the wilderness of Judea, "Repent, for the kingdom of heaven is at hand! Prepare the way of the Lord; make His paths straight," echoing the words of the prophet Malachi,[16] His heart began to pound. "Was this the time? Was He really the one?" Many "messiahs" had come and gone before Him. All had thought that they were Israel's liberation, but proved to be just thieves and robbers, leaving the people drowning in disappointment and despair. Was He ready to walk the prophetic path that lay before Him? He was under no illusion as to where it would end. The words of the prophet Isaiah were engraved in His heart:

> *He was despised and rejected by men; a man of sorrows, and acquainted with grief; and as one from whom men hide their faces he was despised, and we esteemed him not. Surely he has borne our griefs and carried our sorrows; yet we esteemed him stricken, smitten by God, and afflicted. But he was wounded for our transgressions; he was crushed for our iniquities; upon him was the chastisement that brought us peace, and with his stripes we are healed. All we like sheep have gone astray; we have turned every one to his own way; and the LORD has laid on him the iniquity of us all. He was oppressed, and he was afflicted, yet he opened not his mouth; like a lamb that is led to the slaughter, and like a sheep that before its shearers is silent, so he opened not his mouth. By oppression and judgment he was taken away; and as for his generation, who considered that he was cut off out of the land of the living, stricken for the transgression of my people? (Isaiah 53:3-8, ESV)*

Having made His decision, Yahshua walked down the banks of the muddy Jordan River, His face set like flint[17] to accomplish the purpose for which He was born. His countenance bore the mark of that inner struggle and the determination of His soul. He had us in mind. In the Jews who came to be baptized by John, the Law had done its full work — they came because of their sense of sin and guilt, which the ritual sacrifice of the blood of goats could not extinguish. Sin drove them to the voice of hope. They felt their need for God and the forgiveness of God, for freedom from the consciousness of sin and guilt.[18] In His baptism, Yahshua identified Himself with sinful man; He took upon Himself their sorrow, their contrition,[19] their search for God, and became one in heart with the men He came to save.

To every man comes the moment within his heart and soul of a little shiver of doubt, a faint question mark, the terrible feeling that he may be mistaken, the grim possibility that he may be on the wrong road.

---

[16] Matthew 3:2-3; Malachi 3:1   [17] Isaiah 50:4-7   [18] Luke 7:29-30
[19] Isaiah 57:15; 53:4

Yahshua's baptism was the moment when the last of these questions perished forever. As He emerged from the waters, the voice that He most desired to hear rang out loud and clear, audible for the first time to His natural ears, "You are My beloved Son, in whom I am well pleased."[20] In that moment He knew in the deepest recesses of His heart that His Father was God and He was His Son. He received the utter conviction of the approval of His Father, of the certainty of His will for Him, the unshakable certainty that He was the Son of God, the Messiah of Israel, as revealed in the Prophets.

It was not for the sake of the crowd that His Father spoke in an audible voice, but to confirm in His beloved Son the absolute truth of all that He had understood in His years of preparation, and to give Him the unshakable certainty that He was on course to do His Father's will. His preparation was over and the task had begun. The Holy Spirit rested upon Him like a dove to empower Him for all that lay ahead of Him, beginning with the first test:

> *And Jesus, full of the Holy Spirit, returned from the Jordan and was led by the Spirit in the wilderness for forty days, being tempted by the devil. And he ate nothing during those days. And when they were ended, he was hungry… (Luke 4:1-2)*

It was no accident that the first challenge from the evil one was to His very identity: "If you are the Son of God…" He needed the unshakable certainty of who He was in order to endure this testing. Had He given in to the evil one's taunting to seek His own comfort or glory, He would have sinned and disqualified Himself from being the sacrifice for our sins. Instead, by maintaining His communion with the Holy Spirit even at the end of His physical strength, He overcame the persistent temptations of the evil one, and when He had passed the test in the wilderness, angels came to nourish and strengthen Him.[21]

The test was real, with the real possibility of failure. It was not a performance by God masquerading as a man. It was the very real suffering of a very real man who overcame through the spiritual communion He maintained with His Father in heaven based on the unshakable certainty that He was a son doing His Father's will. That is how He lived His entire life, and that is how He expects His followers to live their lives, overcoming by the means of grace He opened up for them.

Because He overcame as a man, He was able to take man's place in death. On the cross He said, "It is finished."[22] He had finished the

[20] Mark 1:11; Luke 3:22   [21] Matthew 4:11   [22] John 19:30

course[23] He had begun at His baptism, having maintained vital communion with His Father, never committing sin to His dying breath. Never once did He have a complaint against His Father. He knew who He was and what He was to do. Then, in the final moments of His life, the full weight of our sins came upon Him.[24] In that instant, His Father turned His face from Him for the first time in His life. He cried out, *"MY GOD, MY GOD, WHY HAVE YOU FORSAKEN ME!"* Then He went into death — as a man, alone, without the help of His Father — which is exactly what awaits all who die without a sacrifice for their sins. As gruesome and terrible as was His dying on the cross, it was in death, which is unimaginably worse, that He actually paid for man's sin.[25]

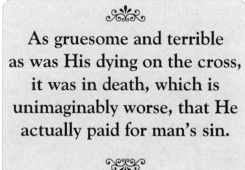

As gruesome and terrible as was His dying on the cross, it was in death, which is unimaginably worse, that He actually paid for man's sin.

His unblemished life was an acceptable sacrifice, the spotless Lamb of God that paid for our sins.[26] Just as He took identity with us in His baptism, utterly committing His life to die for us, so also in our baptism we must be united with Him in His death,[27] utterly committing our lives to live for Him.[28] Apart from the total surrender and abandonment of our lives, we cannot have the unshakable certainty that we are sons of God who are doing His will by the grace and strength He provides. And apart from that unshakable certainty we will not overcome the temptations of the evil one, but will instead seek our own comfort and glory.

There must be a people who will walk in the same way in which He walked,[29] having the same unshakable certainty that He had, in order for the evil ruler of this age to be bound and for Yahshua the Messiah to return and establish His kingdom on this earth.[30] Do you long for that unshakable certainty that you are His son, doing His will in His Body on earth? He lives in every place where His people dwell together in unity, lifting up holy hands without wrath or dissension.[31] That is where He honors His sons who serve Him by the grace and strength He provides.[32] ✿

---

[23] Luke 13:22,32 (ESV, RSV) [24] 2 Corinthians 5:21; Isaiah 53:6,10,11
[25] Romans 6:23 [26] John 1:29 [27] Romans 6:1-7 [28] 2 Corinthians 5:14-15
[29] 1 John 2:6; Colossians 1:10 [30] Hebrews 10:13; Revelation 19:7; Acts 3:21 — This speaks of the restoration of all things in the next age, after Messiah's return, when the promise to Abraham will be fulfilled, restoring the land to Abraham's descendants, ruled over by Messiah and His apostles from the first century, as He said in Matthew 19:28. [31] 1 Timothy 2:8; John 17:20-23 [32] John 12:25-26

Then the Spirit of the LORD came upon Jephthah… And Jephthah made a vow to the LORD: "If you give the Ammonites into my hands, whatever comes out of the door of my house to meet me when I return in triumph from the Ammonites will be the LORD's, and I will sacrifice it as a burnt offering."

Then Jephthah went over to fight the Ammonites, and the LORD gave them into his hands… When Jephthah returned to his home in Mizpah, who should come out to meet him but his daughter, dancing to the sound of tambourines! She was his only child. Except for her he had neither son nor daughter.

When he saw her, he tore his clothes and cried, "Oh! My daughter! You have made me miserable and wretched, because I have made a vow to the LORD that I cannot break."

"My father," she replied, "you have given your word to the LORD. Do to me just as you promised, now that the LORD has avenged you of your enemies, the Ammonites."

So she said to her father, "Let this thing be done for me: leave me alone two months, that I may go up and down on the mountains and weep for my virginity, I and my companions."

So he said, "Go." Then he sent her away for two months, and she departed, she and her companions, and wept for her virginity on the mountains. And at the end of two months, she returned to her father, who did with her according to his vow that he had made.
(Judges 11:29-39)

JEPHTHAH'S DAUGHTER

The tragic story of Jephthah's daughter has troubled Christians and Jews alike for thousands of years. Countless commentaries have attempted to explain away the haunting specter of Jephthah killing his precious only child and offering her up as a burnt offering. They say it was a *rash*[1] vow, which God would not expect Jephthah to literally fulfill. Surely God wouldn't condone human sacrifice, would He?

Jephthah's "Rash" Vow

Consider how the story begins: "Then the Spirit of the LORD came upon Jephthah… and Jephthah made a vow to the Lord." How then could it have been a *rash* vow unless we are ready to accuse God Himself of being rash? But why would the Spirit of God inspire a man to make such a vow? And what kind of young woman was

---

[1] Rash — done impulsively, without careful consideration.

Jephthah's daughter to willingly give herself to such a fate? These are very deep questions whose answers touch the very foundation of God's eternal purpose for mankind.

While it is doubtful that Jephthah expected his daughter to be what would come first out of his house when he returned from battle, considering his reaction when he saw her, neither can it be assumed that he was confident it would be a sheep or a goat instead. God chose Jephthah because of his heart, knowing that he would withhold nothing from Him, not even his only child. And when His Spirit came upon Jephthah to deliver Israel from being snuffed out as a nation, Jephthah's response confirmed why he was chosen.[2] He would give anything to secure the victory, and God saw fit to test him. Does that remind you of someone else?

> *After these things God tested Abraham and said to him, "Abraham!" And he said, "Here am I." He said, "Take your son, your only son Isaac, whom you love, and go to the land of Moriah, and offer him there as a burnt offering on one of the mountains of which I shall tell you." ...*
>
> *Then they came to the place of which God had told him, Abraham built the altar there and laid the wood in order and bound Isaac his son and laid him on the altar, on top of the wood. Then Abraham reached out his hand and took the knife to slaughter his son.*
>
> *But the angel of the LORD called to him from heaven and said, "Abraham, Abraham!" And he said, "Here am I." He said, "Do not lay your hand on the boy or do anything to him, for now I know that you fear God, seeing you have not withheld your son, your only son, from Me."* (Genesis 22:1,2,9-12)

There can be no doubt that Abraham was actually in motion to take his son's life, being fully persuaded that his God was able to raise Isaac from the dead to fulfill His promise.[3] But God did not require it of him, providing instead a ram for the burnt offering. It was a great test, and Abraham passed the test. So why did God not provide a substitute for Jephthah's daughter?

[2] Hebrews 11:32 [3] Hebrews 11:17-19

164

He wanted to teach us something very important about vows, about love, and about a willing sacrifice.

Jephthah had made a vow to his God, and a vow is not to be broken:

If a man vows a vow to the LORD, or swears an oath to bind himself by a pledge, he shall not break his word. He shall do according to all that proceeds out of his mouth. (Numbers 30:2)

There is an old and true expression that very few people in this day and age understand: *A man is only as good as his word.* Gone are the days when men could have confidence in an oral agreement sealed merely by a handshake. Today, words are cheap and carry little weight unless they are backed up by a written legal contract, and that with economic teeth behind it. But God does not change, nor will He forget a single word that we speak:

"I tell you, on the Day of Judgment men will give account for every careless [useless] word they speak, for by your words you will be justified, and by your words you will be condemned." (Matthew 12:36-37)

The sobering truth is that a man's worth is measured by his faithfulness to keep his word, for he is made in the image of the One whose word is true and unchangeable.[4] A man who breaks his word misrepresents his Creator and undermines the very foundations of human civilization. This understanding escapes modern man, but it was not lost on Jephthah… or on his daughter.

For Jephthah to shrink back from fulfilling his vow would have broken something in the core of his being. It was not a matter of his own personal pride, but of the very fabric of his human-ity, and not only his, but also the integrity of his people. Even his great love for his daughter could not nullify his vow to his God.

Jephthah's daughter was a completely willing sacrifice. She did not whimper or bemoan the outcome of her father's vow. Who is like unto her? The Bible does not record her name, and she would be content just

[4] Psalm 119:160; John 17:17

to be identified by her father's name. But we will call her *Ishshah*, a Hebrew word that means both *woman* and *burnt offering*.

Ishshah did not consider her own life to be worth more than her father's integrity. She loved him more than her own life. To shrink back from giving up her life to enable him to fulfill his vow would break something in the core of her being. She would not be able to go on living. Even her request for two months' time to "weep over her virginity" was not for her own personal loss, but for grief over the fact that she would not be able to give him grandchildren. It was there that she found her identity as a woman — to raise up godly offspring and pour her life into them — and once she had closed that door in her heart, she presented herself to her father to give her life as a burnt offering.

Jephthah proved to be a true son of Abraham who trained up his daughter in the way of the LORD, and Ishshah proved to be a daughter who had received her father's heart. She would withhold nothing from him, just as he would withhold nothing from his God. What was the significance of her short life? Why is this short and seemingly tragic story preserved for us?

God's "Rash" Vow

There is another Father who made a grave vow, which if He did not fulfill it, would result in the literal ripping apart of His very being. It was God Himself, and His vow was to Abraham:

> And He said to him, "I am the LORD who brought you out from Ur of the Chaldeans to give you this land to possess."
>
> But he said, "O Lord GOD, how am I to know that I shall possess it?"
>
> He said to him, "Bring me a heifer three years old, a female goat three years old, a ram three years old, a turtledove, and a young pigeon." And he brought him all these, cut them in half, and laid each half over against the other… And when birds of prey came down on the carcasses, Abram drove them away. As the sun was going down, a deep sleep fell on Abram. And behold, dreadful and great darkness fell upon him…
>
> When the sun had gone down and it was dark, behold, a smoking fire pot and a flaming torch passed between these pieces. On that day the LORD made a covenant with Abram, saying, "To your offspring I give this land, from the river of Egypt to the great river, the river Euphrates, the land of the Kenites, the Kenizzites, the Kadmonites, the Hittites, the Perizzites, the Rephaim, the Amorites, the Canaanites, the Girgashites and the Jebusites." (Genesis 15:7-21)

What was the significance of this peculiar animal sacrifice? How did it answer Abram's question, "How am I to know that I shall possess it?"

The shocking solution to this puzzle is found in a passage far away in the prophecy of Jeremiah:

> *And the men who transgressed My covenant and did not keep the terms of the covenant that they made before Me, I will make them like the calf that they cut in two and passed between its parts… I will give them into the hand of their enemies and into the hand of those who seek their lives. Their dead bodies shall be food for the birds of the air and the beasts of the earth.* (Jeremiah 34:18,20)

This passage shows the terms of a very serious kind of covenant, something that was understood by the ancient Hebrews. The initiator of this kind of covenant would pass between the halves of an animal split in two, saying by that action, "May it happen to me just as to this animal if I do not keep my promise."

In other words, God answered Abram's question by saying, "If I do not give your descendants this land, may the fate of these animals come upon Me." God Himself would be torn asunder! It is no exaggeration to say that the fate of the universe is at stake in what happens to this land.

So considering what is at stake, why hasn't God already fulfilled His promise? Some might say, "What's the big deal? The Jews are already back on their land!" Well, for one thing, take a closer look at the boundaries. The Jews are occupying only a small portion of that promised land, and it seems rather unlikely that they are going to gain the rest of it anytime soon, by force of arms or any other means. But even if they or their allies conquered the entire Arab world and seized their land, still it would not be the blessing of God, for God, who does not change, has made it very clear what is required of Abraham and his descendants in order for Him to give them the land:

> *For I have chosen him, that he may command his children and his household after him to keep the way of the LORD by doing righteousness and justice, so that the LORD may bring to Abraham what He has promised him.* (Genesis 18:19)

The Bible records very clearly that Abraham's descendants after Jacob did not do this. They rebelled and gave themselves to all manner of idolatry, injustice, and wickedness. Because of their disobedience, God could never deliver the entire land into their hands, and even had to drive them out of the portion they once possessed, swearing that He would not bring them back to the land until...[5]

> "... you return to the LORD your God and obey His voice, according to all that I command you today, you and your children, with all your heart and with all your soul..." (Deuteronomy 30:2)

No one who knows anything about how the Jews got back to Palestine, and what their moral and spiritual life is like there, can be under any illusion as to what force is sustaining them. It is certainly not God's blessing on account of their national repentance and righteousness! No, it will take something of an entirely different nature to enable this heavenly Father to fulfill His vow. It will take a *woman* like Jephthah's daughter. It will take an *Ishshah* — a willing burnt offering.

The Daughter of Zion

That is why Israel is so often called the "daughter of Zion" in the Scriptures,[6] and the church, as the spiritual Israel, is characterized as a virgin betrothed to Messiah.[7] There is a purity of devotion, a

There is a purity of devotion, a self-sacrificing quality, that is so pleasing in a woman who finds her identity in serving her father or husband. That is an unpopular point of view today, but, like it or not, it is clearly the viewpoint of the Bible.

self-sacrificing quality, that is so pleasing in a woman who finds her identity in serving her father or husband. That is an unpopular point of view today, but, like it or not, it is clearly the viewpoint of the Bible. Our heavenly Father has always desired a people for His own possession who would be like a pure virgin daughter to Him, to be prepared as a bride for His Son, Yahshua[8] the Messiah. And just as He willingly gave up His life as a sacrifice for her, she also must willingly give up her life for Him, to bring about His Father's will on the earth.

---

[5] Please see all of Deuteronomy chapters 28 through 30 for the full context.
[6] Zephaniah 3:14; Zechariah 9:9; Matthew 21:5 [7] 2 Corinthians 11:2 [8] See *The Name Above All Names* on page 151.

This is not just the pretty symbolic language of the Scriptures, but must be the practical reality of every disciple's life. The apostle Paul understood this and continually called the first-century believers to this standard:

> I beseech you therefore, brethren, by the mercies of God, that you **present your bodies a living sacrifice**, holy, acceptable to God, which is your **reasonable service**. And do not be conformed to this world, but be transformed by the renewing of your mind, that you may prove what is that good and acceptable and perfect will of God. (Romans 12:1-2)

They were each to daily[9] present their individual bodies as one corporate sacrifice, as one *Ishshah*, to bring about the will of their Father. If anyone is not willing to present himself in total surrender, it shows that he is not ready to have communion with Him.

Paul made it clear in his defense before King Agrippa that their *reasonable service* had everything to do with bringing about God's promise to Abraham:

> And now it is for the hope of the promise made by God to our forefathers that I stand here on trial, which promise our twelve tribes, by devotedly serving Him day and night, hope to see fulfilled for them. It is for this hope, your Majesty, that I am accused by the Jews. (Acts 26:6-7)

By "our twelve tribes" Paul meant the church, the spiritual Israel that was being raised up largely from among the Gentiles, to be a light to all nations, showing them the fruit of being truly connected to the God of Abraham, Isaac, and Jacob. Paul knew all too well that Abraham's physical descendents had not produced that fruit, therefore what Yahshua had said to the religious leaders in Jerusalem had come upon them:

> "Therefore I say to you, the kingdom of God will be taken from you and given to a **nation** bearing the fruits of it." (Matthew 21:43)

That nation to whom the kingdom would be given would be the fulfillment of this prophecy of Isaiah, which Paul applied to his life's work:[10]

> He says, "It is too small a thing that You should be My Servant to raise up the tribes of Jacob and to restore the preserved ones of Israel; I will also make You a light to the nations so that My salvation may reach to the end of the earth." (Isaiah 49:6)

The "You" here is the Messiah, and His Body, the twelve-tribed spiritual Israel[11] that He would raise up through His twelve apostles, to be

---

[9] Luke 9:23; Acts 2:46; 1 Corinthians 15:31; Hebrews 3:13; 10:24-2
[10] Acts 13:47; Romans 9 - 11   [11] See also 1 Peter 2:9-10

a light to the nations so that His salvation would reach the ends of the earth. But if you look two verses later, you will see the *purpose* of the restoration of a twelve-tribed spiritual nation:

> *Thus says the LORD, "In a favorable time I have answered You, and in a day of salvation I have helped You; and I will keep You and give You for a covenant of the people, to restore the land, to make them inherit the desolate heritages." (Isaiah 49:8)*

This new spiritual Israel must bear the fruit that old Israel did not bear, fulfilling the Law and the Prophets[12] *for them* (including Genesis 18:19, quoted above), so as to move Abraham's physical offspring to jealousy,[13] ultimately bringing a remnant of them to repentance.[14] This will release their God to righteously give them their desolate heritage in the next age,[15] the enemy-free land He promised to Abraham, so that God Himself is not cursed along with the land.[16]

Sadly, just as old Israel, the new spiritual Israel that came to birth in the first century, went astray[17] and ceased to bear the fruit of the Kingdom. Though she began as a pure virgin, characterized by self-sacrificing love and devotion,[18] she became a harlot, characterized by selfishness, strife, jealousy, immorality, and violence, using worldly power and influence to sustain herself.[19] Rather than being a light to the nations, she has brought great darkness to the whole earth, though smugly, she calls it light.[20] That is why, after almost 2000 years, Messiah has not returned, and the Father's promise to Abraham has not been fulfilled.

So now the earth's darkest hours are upon us. Fallen man and fallen religion are steering a steady course toward the utter destruction of the earth and its inhabitants and, unthinkably, of its Creator. Unless there is a rebirth of that spiritual Israel that will bear the fruit of the Kingdom, truly being a light to the nations so that His salvation can reach the ends of the earth, then there is no hope.

Jephthah's Daughter Reborn

In the days of old Israel's decline, the prophet Malachi had foretold:

> *"Behold, I will send you Elijah the prophet before the great and awesome day of the LORD comes. And he will turn the hearts of fathers to their children and the hearts of children to their fathers, lest I come and strike the land with a curse." (Malachi 4:5-6)*

---

[12] Matthew 5:17 [13] Deuteronomy 32:21; Romans 10:19; See also the article *Foolish Nation*, on our web site: *http://www.twelvetribes.org/publications/foolish-nation.html* [14] Zechariah 12:10; 13:8-9; Romans 11:12-15 [15] Matthew 19:28 [16] Malachi 4:6 [17] 2 Corinthians 11:3 [18] Acts 2:42-47; 4:32-35 [19] Revelation 17:1-5; 18:2-5; Isaiah 1:21 (Ironically, the time on earth called "The Dark Ages" is when the fallen church held the greatest influence and power.) [20] Matthew 6:23; John 9:41

The first coming of "Elijah" was through the ministry of John the Baptist,[21] who prepared the way for the Messiah's first coming, piercing the hearts of sincere Israelites to see that they had drifted far from the heart of their God. But after John the Baptist had lived and died, Yahshua still said, "Elijah does come, and he will restore all things."[22] What did He mean? What His disciples could not understand then is abundantly clear now: Through Yahshua, the Holy Spirit spoke of a time far in the future when the religious system again would be utterly fallen and "Elijah" would come again to prepare a people for Messiah's second and final coming.

That prophetic voice is on the earth again today to restore all things before the great and awesome day of the LORD comes. It is nothing less than the rebirth of the holy nation of twelve tribes — an entire people with the heart of Jephthah's daughter, each one living a life of self-sacrifice by laying down his life daily to serve his Father by serving one another. The first thing to be restored was the true gospel, the Good News of the King- dom, that gave us the faith to utterly and literally abandon our old lives in this world[23] because it revealed to us the true Messiah and His kingdom, worth more than our own lives. Our death in baptism was as real as it could be, short of our physical death. When we truly died with Yahshua in baptism,[24] we were truly forgiven, and only then could we present our bodies as an acceptable sacrifice.[25]

> Yahshua did not come just to help us out of trouble, but to take over our life. He bought and paid for us by dying and receiving the wages of our sin in death, so the total surrender of our lives is the only reasonable response.

A burnt offering is an offering that is given without any reservations. The entire personality is consumed on the altar, as in the example of our Master Yahshua. He did not come just to help us out of trouble, but to take over our life. We are His purchased possession. He bought and paid for us by dying and receiving the wages of our sin in death, so the total surrender of our lives is the only reasonable response.

This true gospel restores the true church: the community that resulted when we all gave up everything[26] — possessions, homes, jobs, unwilling relatives, etc. — and clung to one another in love and gratitude

[21] Luke 1:17; Matthew 11:14   [22] Matthew 17:10-12; Mark 9:11-12
[23] John 12:25-26   [24] Romans 6:4-5   [25] Romans 12:1-2   [26] Luke 14:26-33; Mark 10:28-30

for our salvation. This common life together gives us the practical daily context for loving one another just as our Master loved us,[27] for being purified and healed of all our selfish ways,[28] and for growing to full stature in every aspect of our personalities[29] to be made ready as a bride for Him.[30]

But most importantly, the Spirit we have received is turning the hearts of the fathers to their children, and the hearts of the children to their fathers, to fulfill Genesis 18:19 so that our faith and vision does not die after one or two generations. We are raising sons and daughters to have the heart of Jephthah's daughter, not living for themselves, but finding joy in laying down their lives day and night to bring about our Father's will on the earth.

We know that our Master will not return until He has a people on the earth who have put all of His enemies underfoot[31] — that is, the spiritual forces that work through our iniquities, fears, and selfish desires, seeking to divide and thus destroy us. And we know He will not return until He has a people who are keeping the righteous requirement of the Law by the Spirit He has given us.[32] When the light of that spiritual life empowers the Gospel of the Kingdom to be preached throughout the whole earth as a witness to all nations, then the end of the age will come,[33] and Yahshua the Messiah will return to restore the promised land, enemy-free, to Abraham's natural offspring,[34] fulfilling the promise of His Father.[35]

All this can only come about when our Father has a people with the heart of Jephthah's daughter who no longer live for themselves, but for the One who died and rose again on their behalf.[36] He will be pleased with the "burnt offering" of their lives, and will give them the grace to become that spotless bride for whom His Son will gladly return. If this prophetic vision stirs your heart, and you hate your life in this world, please come and help us bring this evil age to an end. ✻

Therefore I urge you, brethren, by the mercies of God, to present your bodies a living and holy sacrifice, acceptable to God, which is your reasonable service of worship. And do not be conformed to this world, but be transformed by the renewing of your mind, so that you may prove what the will of God is, that which is good and acceptable and perfect. (Romans 12:1-2)

---

[27] John 13:34-35 [28] 1 John 3:2-3; James 1:21 [29] Ephesians 2:10; 4:11-16
[30] Ephesians 5:26-27; Revelation 19:7-8 [31] Hebrews 10:13 [32] Romans 8:4; Matthew 5:17 [33] Matthew 24:14; Isaiah 49:6 [34] Acts 3:21; Matthew 19:28; Isaiah 49:8 [35] Genesis 15:18-21 [36] 2 Corinthians 5:14-15

CALLED TO BE SAINTS

Growing up as a Catholic, the word saint only brought to mind spooky-looking figures dressed in robes, with halos around their heads, each with his own particular realm of authority to answer prayers.

Sainthood was a classification out of reach of ordinary people, reserved only for the most devout Catholics who were so holy they could perform miracles even after they were dead. In fact, most of those considered saints had that honor bestowed on them long after their deaths.

Nothing could be further from the truth of what the Apostles taught about becoming a *saint*. On the contrary, *all* believers in the Son of God are *called to be saints*, and the earnest expectation of the Apostles was that *all* would attain to that calling *during their lifetime*. That transformation from helpless sinner to steadfast saint can only occur in a set-apart place where all who believe live together and share all things in common, as the first disciples did in Acts 2:44.

There is a secret hidden in plain sight in the beginning of Paul's first letter to the church in Corinth. Its radical implications are overlooked simply because the life it takes for granted is completely foreign to the vast majority of Christians, yet it reveals the very pattern of discipleship which this apostle considered normal:

> To the church of God that is in Corinth, to those sanctified in Christ Jesus, *called to be saints* together with all those in every place who call upon the name of our Lord Jesus Christ, both their Lord and ours. (*1 Corinthians 1:2*)

Paul understood that *all* believers are called to be *saints*, that is, *holy* men and women who are completely devoted to God and who have been purified from anything unclean in His sight. But he also understood that one cannot become a saint *alone*, but only *together* with all those in every place who call on the *same* Lord.[1] That is why they must first be *sanctified*, which means *set apart* from fellowship with the world and brought into fellowship with God *in Christ Jesus* — in the *place* where He dwells.

There are three foundational words Paul uses here that are essential for us to understand or we will completely *misunderstand* and *misapply* everything else Paul says in his letters.[2] These words are *sanctified*,[3] *saint*,[4] and *place*.[5]

---

[1] Not *another* Jesus, as some of the Corinthians called upon later (2 Corinthians 11:4).   [2] As many have done, to their own destruction (2 Peter 3:16).   [3] *hagiazo*, #37 in *Strong's Concordance*   [4] *hagios*, #40 in *Strong's*   [5] *topos*, #5117 in *Strong's*

As for the Saints who are on the Earth[6]

First, let's establish the objective of discipleship, which Paul made crystal clear in his letter to Titus:

> *...who gave Himself for us to redeem us from all lawlessness and to purify for Himself a people for His own possession who are zealous for good works. (Titus 2:14)*

Yahshua[7] gave up His life to obtain "a people" for His own possession. His objective was *not* just to save individuals who continue to live independent lives, much the same as all the other decent people in the world except for their new-found personal conviction and a religious gathering to attend on Sunday. "A people," according to Webster's dictionary, is a body of persons that are united by a common culture, tradition, or sense of kinship, having a common language, institutions, and beliefs. Therefore, Yahshua's people must be a recognizable body having the same culture, traditions, structure, and beliefs, who are being purified from all that is foreign to His nature. As Jude wrote,[8] it's all about "our *common* salvation," because Yahshua is not going to return until this *people* is made ready, like a spotless Bride prepared for her King.[9]

The Apostle Peter also wrote about "a people for His own possession" in a way that sheds more light on the objective Yahshua had in mind as He was suffering on the cross:[10]

> *But you are a chosen race, a royal priesthood, a holy nation, a people for His own possession, that you may proclaim the excellencies of Him who called you out of darkness into His marvelous light. (1 Peter 2:9)*

He was after a *holy nation*, that is, a spiritual nation of *holy* ones (*saints*) who would no longer live for themselves, but for Him who died, and went into death, and rose again on their behalf.[11] They are a full-time royal priesthood of twelve tribes who serve Him night and day,[12] daily offering their bodies as one living sacrifice,[13] daily laying down their lives for one another out of love for Him.[14] Because of their sincere and whole-hearted devotion to Him they have the expectation of being made like Him *in this life* as they give themselves to the purifying fire of their life together.[15]

Sanctified in Christ Jesus

There is not the slightest possibility of this objective coming about apart from the *sanctification* Paul wrote of in 1 Corinthians 1:2, and which he also described explicitly in his second letter to the Corinthians:

[6] Psalm 16:3   [7] *Yahshua* is the original Hebrew name of the Son of God; see *The Name Above All Names* on page 151.   [8] Jude 1:3   [9] Revelation 19:7-8; Ephesians 5:27   [10] Hebrews 12:2   [11] 2 Corinthians 5:15   [12] Acts 26:7   [13] Romans 12:1-2   [14] 1 John 3:14,16   [15] 1 John 3:2

Therefore go out from their midst, and be separate from them, says the Lord, and touch no unclean thing; then I will welcome you, and I will be a father to you, and you shall be sons and daughters to Me, says the Lord Almighty. (2 Corinthians 6:17-18)

To be "sanctified in Christ" means to separate yourself from fellowship with the world and be immersed into the fellowship of His people through baptism into His Body, which is a people who dwell together in unity as a light to the surrounding world.[16] That is where you receive the Spirit of adoption as a son or daughter that enables you to truly cry, "Abba!" (that is, *Father*),[17] being truly "born again" into God's family, where you can be *fathered* by Him through His people. As Yahshua promised His first disciples who left everything and followed Him:

Truly, I say to you, there is no one who has left house or brothers or sisters or mother or father or children or lands, for my sake and for the gospel, who will not receive a hundredfold now in this time — houses and brothers and sisters and mothers and children and lands — with persecutions, and in the age to come eternal life. (Mark 10:29-30)

Yahshua's radical gospel of forsaking everything is the means by which we are *sanctified* (set apart) from all that is common and brought into one of the holy *clusters* where our new brothers and sisters and mothers and fathers abide together in the Vine. Yahshua told His apostles that He was the Vine and they were the branches,[18] and if they would abide in Him, they would bear abundant fruit. To abide in Him meant to keep His commandments,[19] and He commanded them to make disciples, teaching them to obey everything He had commanded them.[20] And that is what they did.

The fruit of the Vine is the *clusters* that come forth from the vitally connected branches — and what rich clusters came forth on the day of Pentecost! Three thousand people were saved, forming many clusters throughout the city of Jerusalem as everyone left behind their old lives and clung together, drinking in the nourishment that came from the branches, that is, the apostles:

---

[16] They dwell where God has commanded the blessing of eternal life: "where brothers dwell together in unity" (Psalm 133:3). [17] Romans 8:15,23; 9:4; Galatians 4:5; Ephesians 1:5 [18] John 15:5 [19] John 15:10 [20] Matthew 28:19-20

So those who received his word were baptized, and there were added that day about three thousand souls. And they devoted themselves to the apostles' teaching and fellowship, to the breaking of bread and the prayers. And awe came upon every soul, and many wonders and signs were being done through the apostles. And all who believed were together and had all things in common. And they were selling their possessions and belongings and distributing the proceeds to all, as any had need. (Acts 2:41-45)

A grape in a cluster that is vitally connected to the vine through a branch becomes juicy and sweet, while a grape by itself shrivels up and dies. In the same way, it is impossible for a person to become *holy* unless he is grafted into the fellowship of Yahshua's people. You cannot become a *saint* — a pure, sweet, ripe grape — while living alone in the world. It is impossible.

In Every Place

As Paul said, we are "called to be saints *together* with all those *in every place* who call upon our Lord Jesus Christ..." It does *not* say "all those *everywhere*" as the *New International Version* and some other modern versions incorrectly translate the verse, as if it were speaking of individual believers scattered *everywhere* in the world. The word *place* means a particular *locality* in a township. It is speaking of a *cluster* of true believers living together in unity (having "the *same* Lord," as Paul stipulated in 1 Corinthians 1:2) in several households in a particular neighborhood[21] — a *community*.

To be "sanctified in Christ Jesus" means to be *where* He is, which is not the slightest bit mystical, but instead very real and practical. He is where "all who believe live *together*"[22] because they hated their lonely, futile lives in this world:

Whoever loves his life loses it, and whoever hates his life in this world will keep it for eternal life. If anyone serves Me, he must follow Me; and where I am, there will My servant be also. If anyone serves Me, the Father will honor him. (John 12:25-26)

In that place where Yahshua's Spirit dwells in His people, where His people dwell together in a cluster, where they give themselves to the purifying fire of living together in unity, *there* the Father honors them with the glory of His Son.[23] That glory is the inner worth that demands the respect of others. There they learn to walk in a manner worthy of

[21] Acts 2:46 — "...breaking bread from house to house..." suggests households in close proximity.   [22] Acts 2:44   [23] John 17:22-23

Him,[24] doing the deeds prepared for them to build up the Body.[25] And in the process, they are purified as their wrong ways are revealed through their constant interactions with each other.[26] That purifying process which happens in the set-apart place where disciples live and work together is expressed in the metaphor of the wedding garment of the Bride:

> It was granted her to clothe herself with fine linen, bright and pure, for the fine linen is the righteous deeds of the saints. (Revelation 19:8)

What a vivid picture of those "sanctified in Christ Jesus, called to be saints together...," and even more vivid is this prophetic vision of the Bride:

> And a great sign appeared in heaven: a woman clothed with the sun, with the moon under her feet, and on her head a crown of twelve stars. (Revelation 12:1)

Here is the fully-formed holy nation of twelve tribes, having the radiance of the sun because she has put underfoot all the spiritual enemies that plague the souls of men. The term *lunatic* is derived from *luna*, the Latin word for the moon, recognizing that men's souls are influenced by lunar cycles, being more troubled when the moon is full. That is why having "the moon under her feet" depicts the Bride fully prepared for her King, for it is written that He cannot return "until His enemies should be made a footstool for His feet."[27]

The Sign of Sanctification

So the Bride being ready for her King will be a "great sign"[28] that a people have been *sanctified* (set apart), and that sanctification has achieved the desired objective of their becoming *saints* — holy ones who are worthy of reigning with their King. This miracle will be able to happen because there are *places* where disciples can be insulated from the defilement and distractions of the world and nurtured in the pure and life-giving fellowship of the community.

---

[24] Ephesians 4:1-3 [25] Ephesians 2:10; 4:16 [26] Community life is the practical way in which so many proverbs and verses "come to life" in the lives of disciples. "Iron sharpening iron" (Proverbs 27:17) will not accomplish the complete sanctification Paul spoke of in 1 Thessalonians 5:23 if it only happens once a week at the men's Bible study! [27] Hebrews 10:13 [28] Revelation 12:1

They are not isolated in compounds, however. Rather, they live together in the midst of the watching world, reaching out in every way they can, and welcoming guests, for how else can they be a light to the world?[29]

There is another very significant sign spoken of in the Scriptures that has everything to do with sanctification. In fact, it is actually the *same* sign expressed in different terms:

> *You are to speak to the people of Israel and say, "Above all you shall keep My Sabbaths, for this is a sign between Me and you throughout your generations, that you may know that I, the LORD, sanctify you." (Exodus 31:13)*

The most profound sign that there is a people who are truly being sanctified is that we are able to have true rest in our souls and keep the Sabbath together in all our dwelling places.[30] This does not mean merely ceasing from the regular work we do on the other six days. The Sabbath is not a day off on which to pursue our own pleasure,[31] like a "relief valve" from the pressures of living and working together all week long. No, the Sabbath is the culmination of laboring all week long to put our spiritual enemies under our feet — the selfishness and iniquity that hinder our fellowship with one another and our God. It is a day to enjoy the sweet fruit of repentance and forgiveness — the unstrained relationships with our brothers and sisters as we share our hearts with one another — celebrating, eating together, recalling what our Father spoke to us throughout the week, walking and talking together, writing letters, enjoying a game of volleyball, and yes, taking a nap.

The Sabbath is a time to be refreshed, even as our Creator was refreshed by enjoying the fruits of His six-days' labor in Creation.[32] And as the Sabbath draws to a close, we gather together with one heart to celebrate the resurrection of our Master Yahshua, and to break bread with thankful hearts[33] — a fitting way to begin a new week.

Such is the abundant life of the set-apart people of God, who are called to be saints together with all those in every such place who call on the name of our Sovereign Yahshua, the Messiah — their Sovereign and ours! ⚘

---

[29] Isaiah 49:5-6 [30] Leviticus 23:3 [31] Isaiah 58:13 [32] Exodus 31:17
[33] Acts 20:7-8 — It was after sunset, on the eve of the first day of the week (Saturday night).

*The word for **community**
in Hebrew is **edah**,
which also means **beehive**.
This word conveys
the way a hive of bees
live and work together
with a common identity.
Bees have no concern
for themselves, but only
for the hive.*
**So it is with the
communities of God.**

LIKE
A
BEEHIVE

Have you ever watched a beehive? It is fascinating seeing thousands of little bees working together to produce honey. As you come near the hive, you can hear an exciting buzz as they go about the many tasks necessary to keep the hive alive. The workers are responsible to collect nectar and guard the hive. The young bees keep the hive in good condition, feed the larvae, and support in other household chores. There is never a dull moment in the busy life of a bee.

This is much like the life that we have. No matter what we do, we love to do it together. Daily we gather to thank our Master for His salvation, and to hear Him speak to us through one another. This gathering keeps alive a genuine love and care for each other. As we work, we take advantage of the daily situations, guarding ourselves from the selfishness and pride that would come in to separate us and take away our love. Our children are a vital part of our life. We not only educate them, but we work with them to accomplish the simple tasks necessary to maintain a family life. Our life is not a dull routine of chores, but is full of the warmth that comes from the sweet fellowship of friends speaking their hearts to one another, celebrating the Sabbath every week, and participating in weddings and festivals.

But there are a few things that differ in our life from that of a beehive. One is that we are not driven by instinct or controlled by something separate from our own will. Each of us is here because we chose to leave behind our own separate lives to increase the life of this hive. Our life is not enclosed like the hive of a bee, nor do we have a stinger to harm any uninvited guests. We welcome anyone to experience our life with us. Please come and see what it is like to be part of a beehive of people expressing the warmth and love of our Creator. 🐝

PLACES WHERE YOU CAN FIND THE LIFE DESCRIBED IN THIS BOOK

VERMONT

The Community in Island Pond
P. O. Box 449, Island Pond, VT 05846 ☎ 802-723-9708

The Community in Rutland
134 Church Street, Rutland, VT 05701 ☎ 802-773-3764

The Back Home Again Café
23 Center Street, Rutland, VT 05701 ☎ 802-775-9800

The Basin Farm
P. O. Box 108, Bellows Falls, VT 05101 ☎ 802-463-9264

NEW HAMPSHIRE

The Community in Lancaster
12 High St, Lancaster, NH 03584 ☎ 603-788-4376

MASSACHUSETTS

The Community in Boston
92 Melville Ave, Dorchester, MA 02124 ☎ 617-282-9876

The Common Ground Café
2243 Dorchester Ave, Dorchester, MA 02124 ☎ 617-298-1020

The Community in Plymouth
35 Warren Ave, Plymouth, MA 02360 ☎ 508-747-5338

The Common Sense Wholesome Food Market
53 Main St, Plymouth, MA 02360 ☎ 508-732-0427

The Blue Blinds Bakery
7 North St, Plymouth, MA 02360 ☎ 508-747-0462

The Community in Hyannis
14 Main St, Hyannis, MA 02601 ☎ 508-790-0555

The Common Ground Café
420 Main St, Hyannis, MA 02601 ☎ 508-778-8390

NEW YORK

The Community in Cambridge
41 North Union St, Cambridge, NY 12816 ☎ 518-677-5880

The Maté Factor Café
143 East State St, Ithaca, NY 14850 ☎ 607-256-2056

The Community in Oneonta
81 Chestnut St, Oneonta, NY 13820 ☎ 607-267-4062

The Common Ground Café
10 East Main St, Cambridge, NY 12816 ☎ 518-677-2360
The Common Ground Café
134 Main St, Oneonta, NY 13820 ☎ 607-431-1150
The Community in Oak Hill (Journey's End Farm)
7871 State Route 81, Oak Hill, NY 12460 ☎ 518-239-8148
The Community in Ithaca
119 Third St, Ithaca, NY 14850 ☎ 607-272-6915
The Oak Hill Kitchen
7771 State Route 81, Oak Hill, NY 12460 ☎ 518-239-4240

VIRGINIA
Stoneybrook Farm
15255 Ashbury Church Road, Hillsboro, VA 20132 ☎ 540-668-7123
The Community in Alexandria
1330 North Pickett, Alexandria, VA 22304 ☎ 703-823-3294

NORTH CAROLINA
The Community in Asheville (Gladheart Farm)
9 Lora Lane, Asheville, NC 28803 ☎ 828-274-8747
The Community Conference Center
471 Sulphur Springs Road, Hiddenite, NC 28636 ☎ 828-352-9200

GEORGIA
The Community in Savannah
403 East Hall St, Savannah, GA 31401 ☎ 912-232-1165
The Common Ground Bakery
801 Egmont St, Brunswick, GA 31520 ☎ 912-264-5116
The Community in Brunswick
927 Union St, Brunswick, GA 31520 ☎ 912-279-0078

TENNESSEE
The Community in Pulaski
219 S. Third Street, Pulaski, TN 38478 ☎ 931-424-7067
The Yellow Deli
737 McCallie Avenue, Chattanooga, TN 37403 ☎ 423-468-1777
The Community in Chattanooga
900 Oak Street, Chattanooga, TN 37403 ☎ 423-752-3071
Common Ground Café at the Heritage House
219 S. Third Street, Pulaski, TN 38478 ☎ 931-363-8586

MISSOURI

The Community in Warsaw
1130 Lay Ave, Warsaw, MO 65355 ☎ 660-438-2541

The Common Ground Café
100 West Highway 54, Weaubleau, MO 65774 ☎ 417-428-0248

Stepping Stone Farm
Route 2 Box 55, Weaubleau, MO 65774 ☎ 417-428-3251

The Common Ground Café
145 East Main St, Warsaw, MO 65355 ☎ 660-438-2581

COLORADO

The Community in Manitou Springs
41 Lincoln Ave, Manitou Springs, CO 80829 ☎ 719-573-1907

The Maté Factor
966 Manitou Ave, Manitou Springs, CO 80829 ☎ 719-685-3235

The Community in Boulder
583 Aztec Drive, Boulder, CO 80303 ☎ 303-974-5097

CALIFORNIA

The Yellow Deli
315 East Broadway, Vista, CA 92084 ☎ 760-631-1888

The Community in Vista
2683 Foothill Drive, Vista, CA 92084 ☎ 760-295-3852

The Morning Star Ranch
12458 Keys Creek Road, Valley Center, CA 92082 ☎ 760-742-8953

MANITOBA, CANADA

The Community in Winnipeg
89 East Gate, Winnipeg, MB R3C 2C2, Canada ☎ 204-786-8787

BRITISH COLOMBIA, CANADA

The Community in Nelson
2915 Highway 3A, South Slocan, BC V0G 2G0, Canada
☎ 250-359-6847

The Preserved Seed Café
202 Vernon St, Nelson, BC V1L 4E2, Canada ☎ 250-352-0325

The Community in Chilliwack
11450 McSween Road, Chilliwack, BC V2P 6H5, Canada
☎ 604-795-2225

The Preserved Seed Café
45859 Yale Road, Chilliwack, BC V2P 2N6, Canada ☎ 604-702-4442

The Community in Courtenay
7191 Howard Road, Merville, BC V0R 2M0, Canada ☎ 250-337-5444
The Common Ground Café
596 Fifth St, Courtenay, BC V9N 1K3, Canada ☎ 250-897-1111

BRAZIL

Comunidade de Londrina
Caixa Postal 8002, 86010-980 Londrina, Paraná, Brazil
☎ 55-43-3357-1212

Comunidade de Campo Largo
Caixa Postal 1128, 83601-980 Campo Largo
Paraná, Brazil ☎ 55-41-3555-2393

Café Chão Comum
Caixa Postal 75, 86828-000 Mauá da Serra
Paraná, Brazil ☎ 55-43-8812-2280

ARGENTINA

Comunidad de Buenos Aires
Batallon Norte 120, 1748 General Rodriguez
Buenos Aires, Argentina ☎ 54-237-484-3409

ENGLAND

The Stentwood Farm
Dunkeswell, Honiton, Devon EX14 4RW, England ☎ 44-1823-681155

GERMANY

Gemeinschaft in Klosterzimmern
Klosterzimmern 1, 86738 Deiningen, Germany ☎ 49-9081-2901062

Prinz & Bettler Café
Reimlinger Straße 9, 86720 Nördlingen, Germany ☎ 49-9081-275-0440

Gemeinschaft in Wörnitz
Georg-Ehnes-Platz 2, 91637 Wörnitz, Germany ☎ 49-9868-959516

FRANCE

Communauté de Sus
11 route du Haut Béarn, 64190 Sus/Navarrenx, France
☎ 33-559-66-14-28

SPAIN

Comunidad de San Sebastian
Paseo de Ulia 375, 20013 San Sebastian, Spain ☎ 34-943-32-79-83

Sentido Común
C/ General Echagüe 6, 20003 San Sebastian, Spain ☎ 34-943-43-31-03
Comunidad de Irún
Caserío Barracas 88, 20305 Irún, Spain ☎ 34-943-63-23-16

AUSTRALIA

Peppercorn Creek Farm
1375 Remembrance Drive, Picton, NSW 2571, Australia
☎ 61-2-4677-2668
The Community in Katoomba
196 Bathurst Road, Katoomba, NSW 2780, Australia ☎ 61-2-4782-2131
The Common Ground Café
214 Katoomba St, Katoomba, NSW 2780, Australia ☎ 61-2-4782-9744

VISIT OUR WEB SITE: *www.twelvetribes.org*

CALL TOLL-FREE IN THE USA: *888-TWELVE-T (888-893-5838)*

WATCH FOR OUR PEACEMAKER BUSES:

AND OUR PEACEMAKER TALL SHIP:

www.peacemakermarine.com